F  ;

NATIONAL SERVICE
50 YEARS ON

NATIONAL SERVICE
50 YEARS ON

BERWICK COATES

HALSGROVE

First published in Great Britain in 2012

British Library Cataloguing-in-Publication Data
A CIP record for this title is available from the British Library

ISBN 978 0 85704 168 5

HALSGROVE
Halsgrove House,
Ryelands Business Park,
Bagley Road, Wellington, Somerset TA21 9PZ
Tel: 01823 653777   Fax: 01823 216796
email: sales@halsgrove.com

Part of the Halsgrove group of companies.
Information on all Halsgrove titles is available at: www.halsgrove.com

Printed in China by Everbest Printing Co Ltd

Contents

CHAPTER 1	What Is It?	The *raison d'être* of National Service	10
CHAPTER 2	No Escape – or Very Little	How to avoid it	12
CHAPTER 3	First Degree or Third Degree?	University or NS first?	14
CHAPTER 4	Many Are Called	The summons	16
CHAPTER 5	Say 'Aaah!'	The medical examination	18
CHAPTER 6	Home from Home	The barracks	20
CHAPTER 7	New Boys	The new intake	25
CHAPTER 8	Rise and Shine	First day	28
CHAPTER 9	Drawers Jungle	Kit issue	36
CHAPTER 10	Pregnant Ducks	Induction	39
CHAPTER 11	'Toon! Tooooon – shun!	Foot drill	44
CHAPTER 12	Idle Belts	Bull	47
CHAPTER 13	Making a Noise	Bawling, Banging and Stamping	50
CHAPTER 14	Polishing Plimsoles	Physical training	53
CHAPTER 15	Playing for the Regiment	Sport in the Services	56
CHAPTER 16	Just Like John Wayne	Weapon training	62
CHAPTER 17	Little Circles	Fit for service	65
CHAPTER 18	If it Moves, Salute it	Saluting and guarding	68
CHAPTER 19	The Man you Love to Hate	The drill sergeant	71
CHAPTER 20	Why Do You Want to Be an Officer?	Officer selection	74
CHAPTER 21	No Such Thing as Bad Soldiers	Officer training – 1	77
CHAPTER 22	MK 1 and MK 2	Officer training – 2	90
CHAPTER 23	Officers and Gentlemen	Officer training – 3	93
CHAPTER 24	For Real	Active service	96
CHAPTER 25	Holding up the Empire	Foreign postings	118
CHAPTER 26	Falling on Your Feet	Cushy numbers	121
CHAPTER 27	Every Week the Same	The remaining twenty-one months	126
CHAPTER 28	Where Do You Want to Go?	Choice of service	131
CHAPTER 29	The Wide Blue Yonder	The Air Force	135
CHAPTER 30	The Ocean Wave	The Navy	141
CHAPTER 31	The Dividend	The effects of National Service	146
CHAPTER 32	Bring Back National Service	You can't	154

Acknowledgements

No book is conceived in a vacuum. Every book comes from somewhere.

This one began, then, with my publisher, Steven Pugsley. He threw down the challenge – a book about National Service in six months. So I thank him for the smug satisfaction I now feel at having met the challenge. How well I have met it remains for others to judge.

Secondly, I am indebted in particular to two books about National Service which have appeared within the last seven or eight years. The first is by Tom Hickman, and is entitled *The Call-Up* [Headline, 2004]. It has been called the best summary of the subject in existence. So any author writing about National Service, if he has any sense, is going to consult it. And I certainly have not set out to rival it. Mine was a different aim.

The other book is edited by Campbell McCutcheon, and published by Tempus in 2007. It is a miscellany of some of the training pamphlets promulgated by that indefatigable organisation, Her [or 'His', as it was then] Majesty's Stationery Office in the early 1950s.

I have, naturally, picked the brains of survivors, and am particularly indebted to Colin Gamage, Mark Davis and his brothers, and to Don Shepherd, for their memories.

These days, anybody who seeks knowledge on almost anything sooner or later finds himself 'googling'. I am no exception. I have done my share of browsing. Whatever I have been able to gather, from whatever source, I have tried to confirm by the best means at my disposal.

There remains my own memory (which, I am pleased to say, is still pretty sharp on this topic, as is nearly everybody else's when you tap them). I also have a hefty scrap book of pamphlets and revision notes which were handed out to us at the end of countless lectures all those years ago. They were often labelled 'Restricted', but I don't think I am in much danger of betraying vital military secrets to an enemy at this distance of time.

Finally, I thank Yvonne Reed, who runs a cottage industry in proof-reading what I write (her editorial contribution goes well beyond the removal of mere typing errors); and my colleague Stephen Prior, who once again gave generously of his time scanning the photographs.

Berwick Coates

Introduction

This book is about National Service – all National Service. It stretched from 1948, when the National Service Act was passed in Parliament, to 1963, when the very last national serviceman was demobbed.

Two points must be made at the outset.

Firstly, like all books, this one has its limitations; it cannot cover every facet of National Service to the satisfaction of all those who were involved in it. Or, indeed, of any of them. Even those who were not involved in it, who know little or nothing about it, may well spot gaps, oddities, and inconsistencies. This cannot be helped in a book of only about 60,000 words. Something has to go. And a writer is only human.

Secondly, because the vast majority of National Servicemen did their two years in the Army, and because my own experience was military and not naval or aeronautical, I have written largely about what happened to a young soldier. But I have tried throughout to see the subject not so much from the point of view of that soldier as from the point of view of the (usually reluctant) national serviceman. If the mere two per cent who went into the Navy will forgive the pun, we were all in the same boat.

Moreover, there must have been a great deal of common experience between all those who served, regardless of which arm of the Forces. A barracks was a barracks; an unfamiliar uniform was an unfamiliar uniform; a bawling NCO was a bawling NCO. Feelings of inadequacy, persecution, urgency, and depression; of pride, satisfaction, and elation (yes, we felt those too) are universal. Having to do vigorous exercise, being chased, having to tackle daunting tasks, loss of home comforts, even getting up very early in the morning – all these produce similar reactions the world over.

I suggest that memories will rise in the minds of any survivor of National Service who may read this – soldier, airman, sailor, marine; technician, pilot, gunner, cook, pay clerk, signaller, or – perhaps the commonest – PBI (poor bloody infantry). I hope they all find something here with which to identify, and over which (in retrospect, of course) they can chuckle.

If you did not do National Service, here is your chance to dispel a few legends, and find out just a little of what it was really all about. Because it was so long ago, there is perhaps a temptation today not to take it very seriously. Believe me, it was serious all right, for those two and a half million young men who had to do it.

Berwick Coates

Nearly all the photographs in this book are of less than good quality. That is because they were taken in a hurry, with amateur equipment, by young men with a lot on their minds, and with very little technical knowledge or experience. But at least they are real. They have the immediacy of war film footage.

If the subject matter appears partial, that is because this book is only a survey; it is not an encyclopaedia. Of course it cannot cover everything. But it covers the sort of thing that national servicemen had to deal with, wherever they served and in whatever unit they served. If you write about one and take pictures about one, you are writing and taking pictures about them all.

There is also a weighting towards images taken on service overseas, but this reflects both the greater interest in the photograph and frankly of the national serviceman.

List of Illustrations

Summons and Arrival   23

Basic Training   31

Waiting   59

Officer Training   80

Foreign Life   99

Everyday Service Life   104

Personal Accommodation   109

Work   113

Transport and Mud   116

Domestic Life   124

Personalities   129

Provost and Discipline   133

Getting to Know Them   138

Ceremonial   144

Relaxation   151

Leave   159

CHAPTER 1
What Is It?

What the words say – 'serving your nation'.

Is that it? Not quite. After all, anybody who does any kind of job is 'serving his nation' in one way or another, however indirectly – tinker, tailor, soldier, sailor, butcher, baker, candlestick-maker, right down to the 'sagger-maker's bottom-knocker' – a notorious challenger in the 1950s' TV panel game *What's My Line?* – or the 'bunger-up o' rat 'oles' in the wartime radio programme *Garrison Theatre*.

But we don't mean that. We mean something narrower. In the context of this book, 'National Service' refers to all those who have served their country in uniform – in the Armed Forces. In the First World War, all able-bodied young men were called up for military duty. Initially, they were asked. Lord Kitchener's famous poster with the pointing finger ('Your Country Needs You') called countless thousands to the colours.

Unfortunately, such was the casualty rate that within a year, they were no longer being asked; they were being told. The country was subjected to mass conscription.

The legislation lapsed after the war ended, naturally, and the numbers equally naturally dropped. When the Second World War broke out in 1939, the practice was revived, with the National Service Act of that year. You couldn't fight a war without more countless thousands of servicemen to fight it. By the end of the War, millions of young men (and young women) were in uniform.

But we don't mean that either, for all that it is strictly correct.

What this book is about is the *continuation* of this service, when there was no longer any more world war to be fought. The trouble was that our political masters lived in the constant fear that another war (of possibly frightening dimensions) might have to *be* fought.

This atmosphere – or at any rate the edginess of it – might be difficult to convey to a generation which has grown to maturity since the collapse of the Soviet Union. Possibly even to a whole world which is coming to *forget* the collapse of the Soviet Union. We live on a planet dominated by communication media which are dedicated to, or hypnotised by, news. A president trips over his shoelace on the steps of the Elysée Palace, and within seconds it is beamed round the world, thereby spawning world-wide reaction, speculation, prognostication, blogging, tweeting, and general empty-heading. The implication is that we, the public, want, and need, this 'news' – all the time, twenty-four hours a day.

The corollary of this is the growing media tendency to regard anything that is not immediate as of lesser importance. Anything more than a few years ago becomes foreshortened into a vague concept of 'the past' – the modern equivalent of the old primary-school project attitude to 'the olden days'. As these very words are being written, the author is reeling from a news item which claims that the teaching of history is being discontinued in a frighteningly large number of schools, especially the new 'academies', the Government's flagship of 'modern' education. A journalist reported in a Sunday newspaper not long ago that he had recently met two other journalists (grown men in their thirties, professionals) who believed that the Vietnam War was the last chapter in the Second World War.

Well, now – let us forget the rhetoric and explain: why was National Service necessary *after* the War? Because the world was divided into two armed camps – the USA in the West and the Soviet Union in the East. These were the two super-powers. China had not even had its Communist revolution. The whole of the Indian subcontinent (India, Pakistan, Bangladesh) was still ruled by Britain. Africa had next to no independent ex-colonial governments. The European Union was barely a gleam in statesmen's eyes. Europe was split by what Winston Churchill called an 'Iron Curtain': on one side were the democracies of Western Europe; on the other were the 'democratic peoples' republics' ruled by dictators and dominated by the even fiercer dictator, Joseph Stalin in the Kremlin.

That was bad enough. What made it worse was that both superpowers possessed the nuclear bomb. (The Russians caught up soon after the War was over.)

The Communists (so we believed, or were encouraged to believe) were dedicated to spreading what they called 'the proletarian revolution', whether the West wanted to be liberated or not. Their Marxist philosophy claimed that such a revolution was 'inevitable', but the Russians were not above giving the 'inevitable' a bit of a shove in the right direction by way of plots, plans, spies, secret police, propaganda, and general ratcheting up the tension at every opportunity.

The Americans on their side believed that there was a Red under every bed, and poured endless energy, both nervous and military, into keeping the 'Commies' at bay. So for the best part of fifty years, the world lived in the shadow of this massive mutual suspicion and ill-will, in which both sides were quick to push, posture and bluster – at all times keeping a weather eye on the abyss of nuclear war.

It is easy to over-simplify, even make fun of, these attitudes from the safe distance of later decades. But it was in fact a deadly serious business. The record tells us that in 1962, in the Cuban missile crisis, the world did indeed come within a whisker of atomic Armageddon.

This situation necessitated both sides maintaining their armed forces at an artificially high level – just in case. The British Regular Army, it was decided, was not sufficient to assist the Americans in this policy. There was also the small matter of security maintenance in a huge number of colonial possessions all over the world.

Something would have to be done.

So the conscription, which had been instituted at the beginning of a war in 1939, was continued in order to prevent another one, or, if it came to it, to win another one.

And that, my children, is how National Service, as most people know it, began.

CHAPTER 2
No Escape – or Very Little

In 1801, the British Government carried out the very first census. They were appalled to discover that the British Isles contained as many as ten and a half million inhabitants. Small wonder, when one considers the means at their disposal of measuring such things. The London Statistical Society (later the Royal Statistical Society) was not even founded till 1834. Which gives some idea.

There was no such problem in 1948, when the post-war Labour government of Clement Attlee passed the National Service (Armed Forces) Act. They knew exactly how many people there were around, how many of them were of military age, and how to get at them. The Act decreed that all healthy males between 17 and 21 were to be called up for 18 months' service in the Armed Forces. (They were also to remain on the military reserve for a further four years, with a liability to be recalled to 'the colours' in the case of national emergency.) So every young man who reached that age – normally 18 in practice – could expect a communication from His (later Her) Majesty's Government in the near future – the infamous buff envelope.

About the only chance of avoiding receipt of this envelope was to be 'of no fixed abode', a vagrant, a gentleman of the road – anybody who did not fit into normal society and who therefore did not appear on any Government list. There was one other way, of course – crime. If one were really desperate to avoid being shut up for two years in a barracks, one could always find an offence to commit which carried a mandatory sentence of being shut up for two years in a prison – which did not seem to be a particularly preferable alternative. Three years in fact, because one was liable till one was 21, later 26. So to avoid the Army, one had to be prepared to spend all those years in Parkhurst. It seems very unlikely that any young man would have hated the Army that much.

However, that was not the end of the story. Indeed, it was only the beginning. One could normally not avoid receipt of the letter, but there were ways of avoiding, or at least postponing, the service which the letter commanded.

For a start, there were three 'essential services' which were deemed to be so vital that they could not be interrupted even for the needs of Her Majesty's Forces. Put another way, if you worked on a farm, down the mines, or in the Merchant Navy, you were exempt from being called to the colours. Perhaps there exist some statistics which show how many young men conceived a sudden passion for the plough, the pick and shovel, or a life on the ocean wave when they received the buff envelope. But once again, common sense would seem to dictate that the majority were not likely to prefer two years of voluntary muck-spreading, underground living, or seasickness to what the War Office might have in store for them. It is true that some young men ended up on the ocean wave anyway, or up in the wide blue yonder, but they were not to know that at the time. Far and away the greatest proportion of them went into the Army.

So – to put it bluntly – how else could you get out of it?

Religion was one way. You could claim that you were a conscientious objector. These people had had a terrible time in the First World War, when society as a whole recoiled in horror and loathing from what they thought was criminal lack of patriotism close to treason, and base cowardice which put a man lower than the dregs of humanity.

Society had come a long way on the path of understanding and tolerance by 1948, but convincing tribunals of one's sincerity on this topic was no easy way out. You really had to mean it. And be prepared to suffer for it – perhaps in deliberately menial jobs for the required two years.

Quick-wittery or con artistry was another. Try and prove that your health would not stand two years of early rising and square-bashing. If you like, professional malingering. Again, reliable figures are unlikely to exist for those lucky, or brilliant, few who successfully hoodwinked the authorities, because they were certainly not going to publicise their achievements within official hearing. The overwhelming likelihood is that world-weary medical officers, who had seen everything, rumbled 99% per cent of them.

But there were legal ways too.

Besides recognising the value to the country of work on the land, in the mines, and on cargo ships, our masters also understood that the best brains in the country needed developing, to fit them to make their best possible contribution to the nation's welfare and progress. This was expressed by official willingness to allow academic studies to be pursued beyond the call-up age of 17/18. So no pupil sitting for 'A' Level (or its predecessor, Higher School Certificate) was wrenched away from the desk and immured in barracks.

There was no question, of course, but that he would have to do his eighteen months in the end, but at least he would have had time to get his 'A' Levels or his Higher School Cert. under his belt before he did so. (The eighteen months was extended in 1950 to two years, because of the Korean War – in which many National Servicemen were to serve, and with distinction. This was the 'two years' which came to figure in the minds, and the memories, of most of those involved.)

By extension, therefore, it followed that similar postponement could be granted if a young man wished to embark on a university degree course, or some similar study enterprise. Free choice was generally allowed here. You simply filled in a form.

This provoked the great debate which exercised the minds of thousands of eighteen-year-olds: which to tackle first – university or National Service.

CHAPTER 3
First Degree or Third Degree?

As Jane Austen would have observed, 'it is a truth universally acknowledged' that there are certain things in life which nobody, when faced with them, particularly wants to do – like eating your greens, going to the dentist, or learning Latin verbs. Doing National Service was another.

Most young men regarded it with annoyance, dread, fury, wry acceptance, curiosity, or fatalistic humour, according to their temperament or circumstances. It was a rare youth indeed who, noticing from the calendar that the day of his entry was approaching, clapped his hands with pleasure and excited anticipation.

If he really was that keen to do military service, he would have already signed on for three or six or nine years in the Regular Army (or Navy or Air Force). 'Tours', as they were known, were usually, in those days at any rate, of three years' duration, and you signed for the multiple of your choice. It needs perhaps repeating that Britain's military commitments were infinitely greater in the 1950s' than they are now (dammit! – for three years in the fifties we were fighting a full-scale war in Korea. And not against furtive gangs of terrorists or 'insurgents' – whole 'proper' armies. It was because of Korea that National Service was extended from eighteen months to two years).

So the demands of the Armed Forces were that much greater, and the scope therefore for promotion was that much wider. The life of a 'regular' was quite an attractive proposition to the right person. As a famous recruiting poster of the day put it, 'You're Somebody in the Regular Army'. And you were. The total numbers of all three arms were reckoned in millions. Nowadays that total does not reach much more than 160,000 – that is, all three, put together. If the hints of defence officials are to be given much credence, even that figure will drop before long.

Which of course gave an argument to those who didn't want to do National Service: 'They've got all those regulars. What do they want us for?' It was ill-informed and partisan, and largely missed the point, but one can understand why the argument was put. It helped to fuel the antipathy to the whole idea.

Nevertheless, the unpleasant fact had to be faced. For those who did not have promising academic careers, there was not much choice. Perhaps in areas of unemployment, a sociologist might claim that any job – even the Army – was better than none. Maybe. But since the weekly pay for a private soldier was only 28 shillings (£1.40 – pitifully low even by the standards of the time), it might have been wiser to stay at home and hope for something better. However, generally speaking, all those young men who were not in further education or apprenticeships or similar schemes had to lump it. There was no point in filling in any form.

What about those who had a university place waiting for them?

Here again, explanation is necessary, because times have changed since 1948-1962, when NS flourished. A university place in those fourteen years or so was a coveted prize; nowadays it is almost a birthright. In those days there were not that many universities. Obviously then it was much harder to get in. If you did, it was a source of great individual and family pride (except possibly for the privileged few who exist in any western society; they expected it, and usually got it).

So a young man thought very carefully about what to do first – the completion of his studies or his soldiering. There was only going to be one chance; he had to get it right.

Issues look clearer in hindsight. Ignorance always simplifies things. It is tempting to declare from the distant vantage point of the twenty-first century, 'Well, he had to do both anyway. What difference did it make? What was all the fuss about?'

If you weren't there at the time, you can't know. Curiously, a young man's attitude then was equally clouded by ignorance, though ignorance of a different kind. He was not short of information; unfortunately that information was mostly of the saloon-bar-knowall variety – highly suspect, but all there was. There was no internet to look up.

For example, there was the impression given that service in one's school cadet force would gain one preferential treatment when the real thing began. So should our young man from grammar school cash in on this by joining up straight away, while his cadet sergeant's stripes were still hot, as you might say?

Again, it was a common notion that military service made one more 'mature', and it was 'well known' that university tutors looked more benignly on students with more of this 'maturity', and that these more manly students would perform better than their callow companions fresh from their sixth forms.

On the other hand, terrifying stories circulated about the inhuman treatment meted out to NS recruits, which could turn a healthy boy into a cowed, shrinking zombie totally unable to cope with further academic study.

Worse, if you were to be sent on active service, it was 'widely reported' that this could turn a reasonable human being into a conditioned, nerve-jangled killing automaton, totally unfit for ordinary civilian life, never mind a university campus.

The more practically-minded were attracted by the 'bird in the hand' philosophy. If you were going to be ruined by service life, it would be advisable to garner that degree first, while the learning faculties were still in good shape. Once you had BA or BSc or whatever it was after your name, it wouldn't matter what the Army (or the Navy or the RAF) did to you; you'd got it, and no swearing sergeant could take it away from you.

These considerations may sound laughable now, but when you had no reliable means of proving them wrong, they loomed large in the thoughts. You had little else to go on. It was a worry.

CHAPTER 4
Many Are Called

'You are required to report. . . .'

Every young man over the age of 17 received one or these letters sooner or later. It was brief, impersonal, to the point, and wasted no words. It told the recipient which town to go to, which barracks to report at, and which day. As the length of their respective journeys, naturally, varied, there was no specification of the hour.

Here was one of the first puzzles that taxed the brain of recruits, because they made the mistake of trying to explain it in logical terms. Why, they reasoned, were so many young men ordered to travel so far to join up? There was an Army regiment in those days for nearly every county in the realm, yet a Welshman, say, would have to travel over two hundred miles to his joining depot near London; a young Scot would have to make the trip all the way to the Home Counties. (It was to present further unfair problems of travel when these young men secured their first weekend leave. Many of them simply could not get home – and back – in the time, so had to stay in barracks.)

There was little assistance given in the way of travel directions, beyond the bare postal address of the service depot in question. It was assumed that you had the gumption to find your own way. Something of a compliment, perhaps. The only, somewhat bizarre, sign of humanity was the enclosed postal order.

The 1940s and 1950s were the days before routine online banking, credit cards, direct debits, and all the other paraphernalia of electronic financial management – if such a deprivation is imaginable now. Indeed they were the days before the majority of the population used even cheques. Practically medieval. Cheques meant that you had a bank account, and most people didn't. Only posh and rich folk went into banks, and if, by any remote chance, you should ever need to see a bank manager, you put some smart clothes on. Most people earned only about five to eight pounds a week, and so would be unlikely to send money anywhere. If they did the amounts were modest, and they sent a postal order.

It looked a bit like a cheque. You bought it in a post office, for a range of sums – two shillings (10p.), five shillings (25p.), ten shillings (50p.), or whatever. You put it in an envelope and sent it; the recipient took it to a post office, signed it, and got his money. It would show up today among all the plastic currency like something out of the *Antiques Road Show* – quaint, like a groat.

So here was the War Office (or the Air Ministry, or the Admiralty) sending you – very generously – a postal order. Why? Because it represented your first day's pay in Her Majesty's Forces. Presumably it was intended to help defray your travel and other expenses connected with quitting civilian life and joining up. And how much was it for?

Four shillings. 20p. A National Serviceman's weekly wage was £1.40 – which was Oliver Twistian in its meanness even by the standards of the times.

Understandably this 'first day's pay' – in advance – became a somewhat wry national joke. It did not stop the vast majority of the recipients from packing their bags and getting on their trains when the time came.

There will be many occasions in this book – and this is one of them – when one has to stress the importance of the passage of time between the inception of National Service and the present day – over sixty years. So much has changed.

One marked difference between then and now is what might be called the general attitude of the young – from, say fifteen or sixteen to the mid-twenties.

They were more conservative, more conformist, more pliant, more obedient, more plain ordinary than their counterparts today. There were so many more constraints then.

Humanity had just emerged from the most shattering war of modern times. People were poor, exhausted, shaken, relieved to be alive. They had just survived violence, tragedy, shortages, displacement, bereavement, the world turned upside down. They were only too happy to have what they had. Food rationing, for instance, was to last, in some cases, till 1953. The very word 'austerity' is immovably associated with the five years after 1945, when the new Labour Government planned to nationalise everything in sight.

There were few television sets in use. The majority of the population were not on the phone, and did not own a motor car. Foreign holidays were for the wealthy few. In any case, you were not allowed to spend more than £25 a year abroad. The world was stranglingly formal. Men and women always wore hats out of doors. Schoolboys wore caps and girls bonnets. Everybody queued for everything. In a multi-purpose grocer's, for example, you queued for your bacon ration, then you went to another counter and queued for your butter ration, and then you queued again for the things that were not on ration – and so on. Everyone was so obedient and respectable.

There was little student protest, if any. There was no four-letter language on the telly or in the newspapers or on the films. There were no live-ins, no love-ins, no sit-ins, no sleep-overs; no hippies, no yuppies, no trendies, no groupies. Mainline was the four-thirty-five to Waterloo. Crack was a fault in the plaster. 'Gay' meant somebody who was usually in a good mood.

The population in 1948 seemed more credulous and willing to accept than they do today, possibly because they knew less. When that letter arrived, a handful of mavericks considered going to live in the Channel Islands for eight years (you were eligible till you were 26, but not, it appeared, in Jersey or Guernsey), and a few lifelong layabouts may have gone AWOL, but most young men did as they were told, and duly turned up on time.

CHAPTER 5
Say 'Aaah!'

There were a few lucky ones, who had never received a buff envelope at all – the one that told them to report. As has been explained, there had been some resourceful smart-alecs who had set out to convince the authorities that they were unfit for service. As has also been explained, they were duly seen through as easily as if they had been a window-pane.

But there were also quite a few young men who were *declared* unfit for military service. The difference was that this time it was the Army's idea, not theirs. In other words, they had failed their medical examination. Really failed it – something wrong. And not the music-hall-joke complaints, like flat feet; quite serious troubles were discovered, like heart murmurs, or spots on lungs.

Often the news would come as a shock; the patient would have had no idea that he had anything wrong with him. This is partly, perhaps, because diagnostic technology sixty years ago was not as good as it is now. It is also partly because so much medicine nowadays is preventative; in 1948 it was mostly curative; you waited for something to happen and hoped that the doctor or the hospital could do something about it. You went to the doctor with a pain, not an NHS form. (Remember there was not even an NHS till 1948, and it needed time to get off the ground, to seep into the nation's bloodstream.)

There must have been thousands of young men who had never had a full medical examination before in their lives – not one of those chilly, all-clothes-off jobs. When you went to the doctor in those days, and he looked at the troublesome portion of the anatomy, you usually just pulled something up or pushed something down. If you had actually had a full examination, it would have been in the privacy, and comparative comfort, of your local GP's surgery, with carpets and couches and pictures on the walls.

A local drill hall, with bare boards, high ceilings, and wicked draughts, was a stark contrast. So was the company. There were dozens of young men, all complete strangers to each other, about to be 'processed' in, say, a single morning or afternoon.

They were complete strangers to the doctors too. Many of these gentlemen – or so it seemed from their attitude – had been dragged away from profitable private patients (many doctors had strongly opposed the introduction of the NHS) to decide, by a conveyor-belt technique and a series of near-automatic-pilot questions and tests, whether the young, and often acutely embarrassed, manhood paraded before them was likely to be of sound mind and body after two years in battledress, whatever colour battledress that might be.

All this took place with the 'examinees' being dressed solely in their underpants. They carried with them a large medical form. At the end of each examination by each MD, an entry was made on their form, which the patient carried to the next cubicle. The authorities had made a token gesture to minimal privacy by erecting plywood partitions. Whether this facility was for the benefit of the doctors or their patients was not clear.

In the first cubicle, the first test was for eyesight – the inevitable large poster on the wall covered with letters in gradually diminishing font as one's eye went down the list. So far so good. Home ground, as you might say. But, as he moved to the second cubicle, the patient, glancing at his form, was surprised to discover that, with no questions having been asked, he was declared to be of fresh complexion, and his weight was average for his height.

A second doctor dabbed a freezing stethoscope all over his chest and back, and wrote on his form that his emotional stability was 'normal' (during the whole time he was there, he had felt anything but 'emotionally stable').

GP number three peered into his ears and down his throat, and judged that he did not suffer from curvature of the spine. Number four peered at his hands and asked him whether he suffered from ingrowing toenails. He satisfied a fifth that he was not colour- blind, and a sixth that he was given neither to coughing blood nor to bed-wetting.

Finally, a more sociable practitioner cheerily invited him to drop his pants. He walked round the desk, peered down thoughtfully at what was on show, and asked him suddenly to cough. As the blushing boy retrieved his pants, he was asked to leave a specimen of urine on the table at the end of the hall (having of course duly labelled it).

The last embarrassment, however, was yet to come.

After he had fulfilled Nature's needs, and the Army's requirements – and labelled his bottle – he had to wait in yet another cubicle till the doctor whose job it was to take receipt of the slightly warm receptacle (and the medical form, now bursting with startling diagnoses) was ready to receive him.

There might be several people waiting here, in a situation scarcely conducive to conversation: a group of young men, complete strangers, in their underpants, each holding a transparent container with their urine inside it. Since the only thing that individualised them was the contents of these containers, it was difficult to prevent the eyes from being morbidly drawn in their direction, and without other pairs of eyes noticing.

At long last, the sample was duly delivered. Yet another tired doctor glanced at the ponderous diagnoses on the medical form, reached for a small white card, and – usually – scribbled that, after a full medical examination, Peter John Smith was pronounced to be in health grade 'A'.

So now there really was no escape. He was officially judged to be in perfect health, and well able to cope with two years of what, for all he knew, was to be inhuman privation and emotional battering.

He did not feel particularly robust as he walked toward the barracks gate.

CHAPTER 6
Home from Home

The local barracks was a familiar fixture in scores of towns and cities throughout the United Kingdom. Millions of people passed their gates in the everyday course of their lives. Nobody took much notice of them.

It was rather different when you actually had to go in. It was worse when you knew that it would be two years before you would be able to come out again, shake the dust off your feet, and the uniform off your back.

The building was so lofty and forbidding for a start. No homely, curtained windows faced on to the road. The front gates were vast, so vast that they often had smaller gates set into them, like Oxford and Cambridge colleges.

Barracks were also, for the most part, old. Many had been built in the nineteenth century, with grim, soaring brickwork all over the place, like the early mills or factories. Blocks and avenues bore names like 'Alma', 'Balaclava', 'Lucknow', or, worse, 'Waterloo', 'Talavera', and 'Busaco'. That meant that the internal facilities were anything but modern, and had been subjected to endless re-fits and modifications to cater for differing needs as the decades had advanced. But the Spartan architecture and unrelenting internal design stayed constant, and spoke of a bygone age. A great deal of expediency and makeshift had gone on to provide accommodation for the 6,000 recruits who were drafted *every fortnight*, according to the terms of the National Service Act of 1948. That meant that the facilities which had once been deemed sufficient for the Regular Army had to be adapted to cater for an extra 156,000 young men, *every year*, for the foreseeable future.

This was the prospect that faced every young man who looked up at the lofty archway and peered through it across the vast parade-ground inside. Two years… It hardly looked like a home from home.

One of the first surprises he got was to discover that the place seemed rather empty. There were three reasons for this.

The first was that the majority of the regiment wasn't there. The barracks was what the Army called the Regimental Depot. That meant it was the regiment's home right enough, but it was not where the majority of the regiment's personnel lived. A soldier's business was soldiering, and that could take him anywhere in the world. The Depot was where he came when he joined, where he was given his training, and whither he returned to get demobbed. He didn't spend a lot of time there in between.

He could, and did, get posted to any of a score of trouble spots, or even theatres of war. The end of the Second World War did not mean the end of fighting in the world. There were hostilities in the Near East, where the British Government was committed to setting up the state of Israel. India had just become independent, with all the concomitant disasters of mass murder by Hindus or Moslems. Communist terrorists were threatening to take over what is now Malaysia (it was 'Malaya' then). Once the rule of Chairman Mao had become established in China, the garrison of Hong Kong had to be stiffened. There was permanent tension between East and West in Germany, especially when the Russians closed Berlin to surface transport, and the capital had to be supplied entirely by air. The Mau-Mau terrorist outbreak in Kenya absorbed attention, and troops. More terrorists upset the peace in Cyprus, and an invasion (albeit soon aborted) had to be mounted to 'liberate' the Suez

Canal from the depredations of the new Egyptian ruler, Colonel Nasser. Finally, in 1950, a full-scale war broke out in Korea. (These events are not recorded in chronological order.)

As if that were not enough, there were, if not trouble spots, places which threatened to become trouble spots, due mainly to the ill-will of Asian Communists or the rumblings of a host of independence movements all over Africa. Any one of these could mean that British troops could be sent there to keep order, boost a weak government, actually fight rebels, or help out with floods, famines, earthquakes, and refugees.

At the end of the War, the Government had pledged that the existing millions of servicemen would be brought home 'as soon as possible'. The only way to solve the situation was to compel every young man in the country to go into uniform to fill the gap.

Hence, the 'battalion' (the actual soldiering part of the regiment; there could also be a second, or even a third, battalion), as explained, was not usually there.

A second reason concerned what was known as the Permanent Staff. As the title suggests, it meant the people who ran the place, day to day – cooks, clerks, drivers, batmen, telephone operators, sweepers, toilet cleaners, clothing storemen, security guards, and of course the NCO's (non-commissioned officers – corporals, sergeants, warrant officers, and sergeant-majors) and officers who commanded them. Those who had no stripes on their sleeves or pips on their shoulders were known as 'Other Ranks'.

These 'Other Ranks' in the Permanent Staff had settled into their regular duties, and had learned to carry them out with the minimum of effort and fuss. Like everybody who has slipped into a comfortable rut, they did not want to be upset. One of the sure ways of doing that was not to be seen. Keep out of sight, away from the sharp eyes of a straying sergeant or strolling corporal. If you have to move about the barracks, make sure you have a tool or a piece of paper in your hand, and move quickly, with a preoccupied expression on your face. Look busy, and official.

So most of the Permanent Staff were not in evidence either.

That left the remainder of the National Service recruits, and the NCOs training them. A new intake came into the barracks about every five or six weeks.

A lot of the things people think they know about the Army (or the Navy or the Air Force) turn out to be wrong. But they are right in their impression that ten weeks' basic training is a busy time. The average recruit had never in his life packed in so much activity, day after day. (After training was over, that could be a different story, as some members of the Permanent Staff could testify.)

So it was quite likely that the 'senior' training platoon – the ones who had been in for six weeks – would be in the gym, or out in the local park on a cross-country run, or miles away on the rifle range.

The first human being he was likely to speak to was the Provost Corporal, a very superior being in white belt, with white cross-strap, white gaiters, knife-like creases in his trousers, and boot toecaps you could see to comb your hair in.

In fact he rarely got a chance to speak to this lofty creature, because the lofty creature beat him to it. It was blindingly obvious, with his sports jacket, neat tie, light luggage, and uncertain air, who the new arrival was. All the Provost Corporal did was to demand if he was 'New intake?' Receiving a reply in a hesitant affirmative, he would wave a casual arm towards a long, low hut on the edge of the parade-ground, as if further conversation was beneath his dignity.

That led the recruit to the next examples of barracks humanity – the reception committee.

This consisted of a row of young soldiers sitting behind another row of trestle tables, on which languished piles of forms, stamps, and paper-clips. They had hung their berets on the backs of their chairs, on which they lounged rather than sat. Cigarettes were in full view and great profusion. (Yet another example of the difference between 1948 and 2012 – tobacco. Smoke was an inescapable part of life then, especially in the Armed Forces. This was, partly at any rate, because of the War. The constant strain and stress had to be dealt with somehow. There were no pills or shots or tranquillisers; you smoked. And the habit caught on – and spread.)

These young men were out to create an impression. Casualness, worldliness, mastery of the situation. It transpired that they had been in the Army all of twelve weeks. This was their first post-training duty. And very acceptable too.

They had found their first 'skive'.

As already indicated, basic training was a very busy time. After that, what happened to you was very much a matter of chance. If you were sent abroad, at the very least it had the virtue of novelty – new countries, new languages, new horizons. Even better, you could be taught a trade or skill – say, in motor-care or signalling – which could stand you in very good stead for years afterwards. When the Forces taught you anything, they usually taught you very well. If you drew the short straw, you could find yourself on active service.

However, there were many cases where the newly-trained soldier did not get much chance to display his training. He could end up in some dead-and-alive job in a Nissen hut on the Orkneys or the inspection pit of a motor depot in the Midlands, or some remote weather station which made a lighthouse look like the metropolis.

Human nature being what it is, when you have little to do, you search for ways of doing even less. This was 'skiving'. The dictionary defines it as from the early twentieth century, so it was not new. What the Armed Forces and National Service did, between them, was to turn it from an occasional malpractice into a fine art. Everybody, it seemed, kept a weather eye open for a good skive.

These twelve-week veterans were delighted to have tumbled to the idea. It was the public school philosophy all over again, did they but realise it. In such an enclosed community, even a few weeks' experience, which others did not have, bestowed enormous confidence and status. For those on the receiving end of this posturing, it was obvious and perhaps slightly pathetic, but they had no answer to it, because, when you are at the start of your twelve weeks' basic training, and on your first day, those twelve weeks can loom like an eternity. You yearn for such experience yourself. And when you have completed your twelve weeks, you too keep your antennae out for news of a skive.

The virtuoso performers in this activity, or rather non-activity, were the Depot Permanent Staff. It was a treasured skill to make a simple job spin out for twice the required time, and look busy while you are doing it. It was a knack which the Scarlet Pimpernel would have envied to make yourself as scarce as possible, in some distant dormitory or storeroom. It was an inventive development of military camaraderie to arrange for three people to be doing a job which one man could do with one hand tied behind his back. It is perhaps debatable whether, at the height of trade union troubles over demarcation of duties or go-slow campaigns, the shop stewards learned from depot permanent staffs or the other way round.

What did these twelve-week veterans have to do? Show each diffident new arrival exactly where to place his signature on each of the barrage of forms which assailed him as he moved along the row of tables. Any doubt about the exact place was resolved by the stubbing of a nail-bitten, nicotine-stained forefinger on the right spot. A greasy, topless biro was offered, or rather thrust forward. The poor recruit had no idea what he was signing for, or, worse, signing away. He was discovering one of the great universal truths about the Forces – the unassailable importance of a signature. Get a signature, and you're home and dry.

The 'new intake' were now committed. They were in. Grubby forefingers and blotty biros had taken them across the Rubicon.

SUMMONS AND ARRIVAL

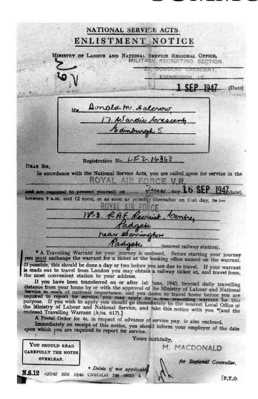

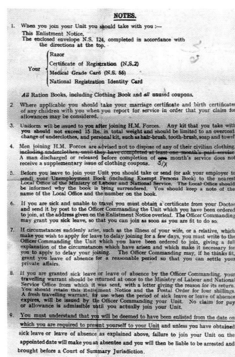

The letter every young man dreaded. Big Brother had caught up with him.

Everyone had just about learned to dress himself so that he didn't look like a sack of potatoes. The dinner-plate berets did at last begin to look berets.

Note the unused mugs placed in line, by now almost from force of habit. And everyone had learned how to make bed-boxes.

The Army usually lived in barracks; the RAF seemed always to live in huts.

Note the webbing equipment squared on top of the lockers, the inescapable (but necessary) iron boiler, and the precisely-arranged brooms – all just like the Army.

CHAPTER 7
New Boys

A barrack room was pretty much what you would expect.

It was long. It needed to be; it had to accommodate anything from eighteen to thirty or more. It was usually tall, especially if it was one of those built to house troops just home from the Zulu War; ceilings were always so high then. Walls were usually done out in some kind of rock-cake yellow or mouldy-cheese green. Lights hung from anorexic flex, with the barest of furnishing in the way of shades. Windows were large, single-glazed, with huge panes designed to conduct the maximum of cold air from outside. Soft furnishings were the stuff of homesick recruits' dreams.

The floor was bare boards, which echoed constantly with the impact of booted feet, often hobnailed-booted feet. In the middle of the room – if you were lucky – there stood a venerable iron stove, which took a good deal of engineering skill to motivate. Coal supply could at times be as capricious as that suffered by Bob Cratchit. When firing on all cylinders, this temperamental device could generate a scorching amount of heat, but only to those quite near. Move away to avoid being consumed, and, on winter evenings, you entered the Arctic tundra.

Beds were, predictably, made of iron. Mattresses were plain, but adequate. Contrary to many worried expectations, sheets and pillow cases were provided, and everybody was soon to be issued with two pairs of pyjamas – quite warm ones actually. Routine issue was two or three dreary grey blankets, plus another, slightly more personable one in Land-Rover green. For some impenetrable reason, this was known as the 'best' blanket, presumably because of its fetching tint.

Between each pair of beds was a locker, lockable, for a recruit's clothes and other personal items. If he was lucky, he might also get a box to put under his bed. This cubic capacity was expected to cater for the whole of a soldier's wardrobe, both military and civilian (though he was usually forbidden to wear 'civvies' until well into his training period, if then). Any other possessions had to go in the locker or the box. That was the recruit's entire 'personal space'. He was expected to keep these two receptacles in good order and cleanliness (more later). He was also responsible for the area around and under his bed – what the Army termed his 'bed space'. It was as if the total area of the barrack room had been divided exactly by the number of inhabitants, and the answer was your 'bed space'. (More of that later too.)

Toilet and washing facilities were in another room. As one might expect with such facilities constantly used by countless successions of inmates, none of whom was anxious to make a home from home, or to stay long in its freezing confines, enamel was chipped; wall distemper was broken and flaky; iron or lead pipes bulged out of walls everywhere; and nobody ever saw a plug present on the end of its chain.

Again, to be fair to the Army, they did in time build some more modern barracks, and facilities in them were more civilised (central heating, for example), but the abiding memory of thousands of recruits will be, I suspect, what I have described.

A new arrival, then, deposited his bag on the first empty, or the most likely-looking, bed he came across, looked about him, tried to stop his heart sinking, and set about making the acquaintance of those who were already there.

Names were exchanged. Gasps were uttered when it was found how far some poor fellow had had to travel. Lugubrious prophecies were exchanged about what was going to happen to them in the next few hours or days. Pessimistic speculation abounded about the provision of bedding and other necessities. And so on. It was perhaps a bit stilted and uninspiring.

Before very few days had passed, however, everybody knew everybody else rather well. Close proximity, twenty-four hours a day, meant that at the end of a fortnight, there was very little you did not know about the others in your room – in physical terms, that is. Looking ahead for a moment, ten or twelve weeks of having to tackle daunting problems, which tested a recruit's psychological resources to the limit, meant that one came to know one's room-mates mentally very well too. There is no way one can put on airs or strike a pose in those circumstances, twenty-fours a day, bunched together, every day, for twelve weeks. The truth comes out.

National Service, if nothing else, was a great leveller. It did not matter whether you came from an urban slum, a Cotswold market town, or a posh Mayfair flat; it did not matter whether your Dad was scraping along on unemployment pay or whether you were born with a silver spoon in your mouth. You were all in it together; you all had to find a way of getting along together; you all had to try, fail, and succeed together.

Not everybody did, of course, and no doubt there were many cases of friction and bullying and general misery which the authorities had to deal with. But it seems fair to suggest that, by and large, the experience for most of those young men, taken all round, was positive.

At the very least it was fair. Everybody had to wear the same uniforms, pull on the same prickly socks, learn the same rules, climb the same ropes, carry out the same rifle drill, go on the same marches, get the same blisters, eat the same food, and live in the same barrack rooms.

There were surprises too.

It did not follow, for instance, that brains and education made one a better soldier. The Forces made demands on a man that were not always to be met by sheer college knowledge or IQ. A newcomer could be a high-powered academic who spoke several languages, but he might turn out to be totally incapable of getting himself up, washed, dressed, his 'bed-space' cleaned, and his locker tidy in the time allowed (which was in fact quite generous). Brains could not cure a bumbler of being incapable of tying two pieces of string together. His neighbours in the room had to help him out – an early example of learning to relate to each other.

Again, it did not follow that an expensive education and rich living made one effete. It is a misconception to believe that if one was rich or posh one had a comfortable life. Anyone who finds this hard to accept should have tried a month in a public school dormitory in the first half of the twentieth century. Ice in washbasins, outdoor swimming lessons in November, cold showers, cross-country runs in gales and storms, relentlessly grey food, near-constant peckishness, and pettifogging rules all taught survival.

There were probably thousands of wartime ex-public-school boys who, when captured by the Germans, found the average prison camp a doddle. Their successors similarly took a National Service barracks in their stride.

Where they were at a disadvantage, of course, was in the Great Game of Life.

For a start, they were vulnerable to the ignorance and jealousy of narrow-minded NCO's (and the Army was not short of those). Poorly-educated corporals viewed their higher exam qualifications with suspicion and spite. By definition, this put them in the classification of 'brains'. If you were 'brains', you were 'superior'; if you were superior, you were ripe for cutting down to size, ideal objects for sarcasm and spleen. In fairness, the general rule was that, the lower the rank of NCO, the worse it was. Seniority did bring more understanding and humanity.

Secondly, they were behind in another vital department. They may have had a tough time at public school, even at grammar school, but both these institutions provided a sheltered existence. They may have learned a great deal, but they did not know much else – like surviving on a council estate, dodging the police patrols, poaching, shoplifting, dealing with large families in overcrowded houses, football terraces, probation officers, magistrates, labour exchanges – the whole of what some today are pleased to call 'the real world'. Even females. Shut away in their near-monastic establishments, they barely saw the other half of the human race. It was a curious mixture of privilege and deprivation.

The members of 'the real world' could run rings round them. They had to become quick learners. Luckily for most of them, they did.

For one thing, many of them were philosophical about the *necessity* of National Service. It was inevitable; it was unavoidable; it was a fair cop. So you made the best of it. Those with university degrees had that much more general experience which helped them to keep things in perspective. It could also make them more critical, and, if they were not careful, this could land them in trouble. Regular sergeants did not take kindly to smart answers.

Some brought skills with them into the Services which helped them to get through. Practical science, for example – how to get out a glass stopper that was stuck in a bottle, which had for several minutes been baffling an instructor corporal. Knowledge of a foreign language – which could be turned to advantage when one received a posting to that country, or to *enable* one to get a comfortable posting to that country. A Welshman could bring his baritone voice with him, and educate his room-mates in the arts of close harmony, which could help many a tedious dark evening to pass more quickly. A keen amateur actor could use his thespian skills to put on a show, which Depot authorities usually viewed with benevolence (anything to relieve the boredom of an evening).

Some simply used their intelligence to devise ways of getting round problems that arose during their training – like the best way to deal with new pimply boots, or the most efficient techniques for coping with the rough surfaces of cap badges. They could gain a certain status by putting these skills at the disposal of others.

Finally, they were not aware of it at the time – well, not in so many words – but everybody – ex-spivs and wide boys, rascals and delinquents, worldlies and innocents, toffee-nose and jack-the-lad – had a shared experience which was to prove invaluable.

The Second World War. Six years of it. Everybody knew about air raids and bombs and unexploded mines. Everybody knew about ration books and shortages and making do and under the counter and black markets. Everybody knew about school air raid shelters and saving paper and carrying your gas mask.

A lot of us had slept in air raid shelters in the garden, played on bomb sites, collected shrapnel which had fallen from the sky in raids or dog fights. We were used to vapour trails and the sound of machine-gun fire. We understood the difference between a Spitfire and a Hurricane. Many of us collected useless information about military ranks and insignia (of modest but practical use when we joined up; at least we would know if we were addressing a lieutenant or a lieutenant-colonel – which could be of dangerous significance).

Many of us had suffered the disruption, pain, and separation of evacuation, and knew what it was like to be thrown, at the age, say, of seven, on one's own resources (very useful in the two years that were to come), and to suffer adversity and unfairness at the hands of our guardians. Many of us had fathers, brothers, cousins (and sisters too), who had served in the Forces, and – worse – who did not come home.

One way and another, we had learned to cope. The War had given us a yardstick; nothing, we hoped, could ever be as bad as that. One might wonder what the modern generation would make of National Service today if it were to return. They would not have that bedrock of experience that we had to see them through.

CHAPTER 8
Rise and Shine

Very few people enjoy getting up early in the morning. (Quite a lot don't enjoy getting up at all.) It is true that one can get used to it, and, once one is up, and dressed, and out, and if the morning is fresh and green, it can be an invigorating experience. One can even feel superior to all those effete layabouts who are still cowering under the blankets without the strength of will even to move.

But the fact remains that the actual act of prising the spine off the mattress and putting the feet on the floor does not have many champions. Very few writers extol the virtues or the enjoyment of that.

This is bad enough in the comfort of one's own home. In a strange set of surroundings, after a traumatic previous day, and surrounded by a roomful of complete strangers, it can be infinitely worse.

This is one of the few legends about life in the Armed Forces that the general public have actually got right. That first morning really is awful. The majority could not remember the last time they had had to get up at six o'clock. Few of them had ever been shot out of sleep by a bugle. Fewer still had ever been subjected to what followed.

Bugles and their raucous reveille do not last long, and it was tempting to try and convince oneself that it was only a nightmare, and all one had to do was snuggle back under the 'best blanket' and all would be well. They had not yet made the acquaintance of the duty corporal.

No doubt different barracks, different regiments, different arms of the services, each had their individual methods for inducing wakefulness among their new arrivals, but the description which follows will do for a typical representation of the process.

The door burst open. The shouting began. The door was slammed shut. This might be repeated two or three times. Again, the duty corporal (or lance-corporal – usually the lower the rank the more its owner 'carried on') would dig into his rich resources of carefully-honed expletive and insult, casting aspersions on every facet of the recruits' personality, background, and parentage.

While this paean of profanity was in progress, the floor would be stamped on, frequently. Windows were opened; the doors of steel lockers were banged; buckets were rattled; the coal scuttle was kicked; broom handles were employed to belabour the iron stove. Feet of beds were tipped up, and allowed to fall. Nothing metallic which could be called into service to make a noise was overlooked. By the end of a few minutes, anybody who was still in his bed was clearly dead, or at any rate totally unable to fulfil military duties; it would be a case for the Medical Officer.

Of course it did the trick. Of course recruits got used to it, learned to expect it, devised ways of dealing with it. Of course, it gradually lessened as the weeks went on, because the corporals realised that their manic behaviour was becoming less necessary. They realised too that they could not enjoy the tempting prospect of deliberately making life uncomfortable for a group of wilting recruits for very long. They would not remain wilting recruits for ever; sooner or later the abuse and the blare would run off their backs like water off the proverbial duck.

In time too, recruits and corporal got to know each other; they had to. It was discovered that corporals could, at times, be quite human. Corporals, if they had any sense or any character, began to take an interest in the soldiers they were called upon to train. If they had neither, recruits would discover ways of expressing their resentment, and the authorities had a trick of looking the other way, so long as overall discipline was not compromised. So corporals had lessons to learn too.

The business of getting up, however, illustrated one feature of service life which the average recruit found a shock, over and above the discomfort, the disorientation, the separation from home life – noise. The same experience has often been recorded by those who went to work in heavy industry.

Any recruit with any sense accepted that armed forces were concerned with fighting, and that guns, and explosions and battle generally, all made a noise. They understood why drill commands were shouted; they had to carry over a long distance. What they were not prepared for was the apparent passion for making a row when, say, the speaker was only inches from the listener.

This is one of the features of service life which many survivors have written about – the corporal, or sergeant, or petty officer, or staff sergeant, or master-at-arms, who thrusts his jowl into the recruit's face in order to correct him, bully him, abuse him, or generally make his life uncomfortable. It has become a legend, a cliché, something every comedy author and scriptwriter has found impossible to leave out of films, shows, programmes about the Armed Forces.

No author will be able to produce a definitive answer to this. No doubt bullying and bawling went on, and no doubt some of it was very unpleasant, and no doubt some of it was quite unnecessary and reprehensible. But it was not universal. The author never had it done to him, nor did he ever see it done to anybody else during his period of training, or afterwards.

It is also worth recording that some of it was carefully designed, and rationed, to produce not misery or belittlement, but effort, discipline, light relief, morale-building, even laughter. In these cases, there was nothing sadistic about it at all. It could be a weapon in the armoury of a good drill NCO.

So – by whatever means – fair or foul – the recruit was up and out of bed, and ready to sample the five-star delights of the barracks wash-room and toilets, known officially and universally, by some alchemy of misplaced euphemism, as the 'Ablutions'.

Depending on the age of the building, the efficiency of the Quartermaster and the cleaning staff, and the general attitude of the regiment or squadron or shore station towards welfare, you found a plug in the basin, a piece of soap, a mirror, hot water, showers, or not, as the case may have been. (In some units, word had it that new arrivals had not even been supplied with bedding at all by the authorities on their first day, and spent their first night on the bare bedsprings, or, in preference, on the floor. But then the Forces were hotbeds of rumours and tall stories.)

You returned to the barrack room and dressed in the clothes you had arrived in, and waited. Logically, you then made your bed – those of you who had not been spoiled rotten by doting mothers or allowed to get into bad habits by neglectful ones. The Armed Forces had something to say about that too.

Recruits were introduced to an inescapable phenomenon of barrack room life – the bed-box. By this time a sergeant had appeared. He gathered his flock round one example bed, stripped it completely of all bedclothes, and set about a demonstration.

He selected, folded, and piled each sheet and blanket so that it was of exactly the same size as the other, and arranged them into a sort of bedding sandwich – sheet-blanket-sheet-blanket. It was about a couple of feet long by about fifteen inches wide. The whole thing was then wound round by the last carefully-folded blanket – the 'best blanket', of course – stacked at the head of the bed, and surmounted by the two pillows.

The sergeant was so taken up with demonstrating the perfection of it that it must have taken him getting on for half an hour before he was satisfied. Gasps greeted the final installation of this masterpiece. My God! Did we have to do this every morning for 730 days?

It was the first of many gasps of dismay at the prospect of what was to come.

The second was the business of haircuts. It was made clear that 'when you come into the Army, you have an Army haircut'. And you did. No doubt different units had different standards, and many were the jokes about the soft treatment dished out to wimpish airmen as opposed to the Spartan no-back-or-sides inflicted on the Marines or the Commandos. A lot of this sprang, as usual, from rumour and tall story, as indicated above. Certainly one never saw the near-shaved specimens that are reputedly common in the French Foreign Legion, which, ironically, would be actually sought out by many young men today. In the end, most young men became used to it and philosophical about it, like the one who sat down in the chair and said to the barber, 'If you can find any hair on the back of my neck, you have my permission to cut it.'

The next hour or two would be spent being given the information necessary for basic survival in a barracks – local geography, local bye-laws (otherwise known as Depot Standing Orders), local personalities, and the shape of the timetable which everyone knew was looming over them for the next ten or twelve weeks. During this time, the squad – or 'training platoon', as they soon learned to call themselves, because everyone else did – had a chance to size up the corporal and sergeant whose acquaintance they had just made.

The corporal was a typical example of the young Regular soldier. A product of city terraced housing. No great brain. No dazzling skills. So no privileged background. Many of them had little or no background at all. He had probably left school with no sixteen-plus qualifications. Quite likely had a succession of dead-end jobs, all of which he had found boring. Then one day he saw a young soldier home on leave – in uniform. (One great difference between 1948 and now: you saw men in uniform all over the place. They were as universal as anoraks.)

He was bowled over – by the soldier's erect bearing, by his smartness (box pleats and all), by his sense of pride and purpose. All of them were so distant and foreign to everything he had known since he had been born. He was down to the recruiting office the next day.

The sergeant had probably started from further back still. The Army (and probably the Air Force and the Navy) was full of them – men in their late twenties who had risen from the ranks with the same quick wit which had seen them rise from the gutter.

At home they had learned to survive in large families, with many of their members on the edge of or knee-deep in petty crime. He had a poor record of academic distinction at school, from lack of intellect, lack of interest, or lack of effort. He had become the despair of schoolmasters, neighbours, local constables, probation officers, and magistrates.

But he was not without resource: a quick wit, a sharp memory (when necessary), light fingers, a sound physique, a raucous voice and rich vocabulary (the legacy of years of street disagreements), and a plausible manner.

To his surprise and gratification, he had found that all these gifts redounded to his credit when he donned khaki (or mid-blue or navy blue). As he won promotion, he became invaluable to his platoon officer. He was able to procure anything, so long as no questions were asked. He could commit to memory the salient features of a training pamphlet, and could perform simple tasks of instruction. He could keep discipline; having been a rogue, he knew how to deal with them.

It would of course be unfair, even abusive, to suggest that every sergeant was like this, but enough of them were to be able to construct this portrait. One could equally build a similar picture of another NCO, a credit to Army, Navy, or Air Force.

BASIC TRAINING

(Left) Grappling for the first time with Shirts angola.

(Right) Kit issue and what not to do with it. The Drawers woollen seemed to echo the old prizefighter days. If they had had to do National Service, perhaps the Three Musketeers would have begun like this.

Learning to wear uniform. Mastering the precise position of the cap badge – one inch over the left eye – and trying the unromantic, square-ended woollen tie.

Why did they make so many young men go so far to join up? These three recruits were forced to travel from Yorkshire, Scotland, and Wales to join a regiment in Kingston upon Thames.

If nothing else, the Army taught you to dress yourself smartly. Everyone had to learn, among other things, how to press trousers.

Not all recruits were beardless schoolboys. Some already had a degree, often two, occasionally three, like this man. He was married too. Note his name written on a carefully "boxed" section of his kitbag, and the equally carefully-boxed "top kit" – the webbing packs and pouches.

A lot of ex-recruits stayed on at the Depot and became part of the training staff. Many of them really did look like overgrown schoolboys. Nice schoolboys, but schoolboys. A purist would insist that this corporal's cap badge could benefit from a slight shift so that it sat directly over the left eye.

Denim uniform made you look a bit like Chairman Mao. Even if you had the collar done up, you had to have a tie on underneath.

A typical RAF training squad. Their particular bête noire *was usually not a sergeant, but a corporal.*

They never thought the day would arrive, but basic training did actually come to an end, and the Army celebrated with a formal photograph. In the front was the Training Company Commander – a war veteran; the platoon commander (a National Service subaltern); two National Service lance-corporals; and the "man you love to hate", the training sergeant (another war survivor – look at the medal ribbons).

It was interesting to see how many ways there were of wearing a beret. By the end of the twelve weeks, one could tell who the wearer was simply by his silhouette.

An RAF recruits' passing-out parade. They had only eight weeks' basic training. For NCO's to produce such a turn-out and performance with raw civilians in such a short time, when you think about it, was quite a feat.

CHAPTER 9
Drawers Jungle

The Army often talked backwards. Large organisations or professions have this trick of being impenetrable. Lawyers talk tortuously, politicians talk interminably, Inland Revenue documents talk incomprehensibly, and doctors talk another language altogether. Priests of the oracle used to talk enigmatically. Well, the Army used to talk backwards.

It became a regular joke among those who had to suffer it, and a regular reminiscence among those who had survived it. So a pair of woollen pants became 'Drawers, woollen, pairs, one'. A pair of ordinary Army boots was translated into 'Boots, ammunition, pairs, one'.

Why 'ammunition'? One of the Great Mysteries which recruits had to grapple with. Did you wear them only when you were carrying artillery shells? Were they to be melted down to make cordite in an emergency? Did commandos store their hand grenades in them at night to keep them dry? The riddle remained unsolved.

Does the Army still talk backwards? The author does not know. Does the Navy? Does the RAF? Quite probably. Because, despite the apparent silliness of it, and the extensive mileage that comedians have got out of it, it does make sense in a po-faced sort of way.

Think of the index of a hefty book. Say, one about Nelson. You will find, for example, 'Nelson, birth'; 'Nelson, family'; 'Nelson, midshipman'; and so on. It will get more complicated, and lead to 'Nelson, battles, Copenhagen, telescope', or 'Nelson, Trafalgar, signal before battle'. The reader has to be able to find the reference he wants, and quickly. He wouldn't find it as easily if he had to look up 'telescope' or 'signal' or 'family', because they are such common words and could have been used a score of times by the author, and it would have been pointless to put them all in the index; quite possibly they would have been omitted altogether, in their own right, as you might say.

By the same token, Army storemen, and Navy and RAF storemen too, had to be able to locate any one of thousands of items at short notice. Therefore, one worked from large to small. So a P.E. singlet became 'Vests, P.E., red, one'. Heavy-duty industrial gloves became 'Gloves, wire, protecting'. Like so many things in service life which might strike the recruit as bizarre, and which causes the general public to chuckle in a slightly superior way, there was a reason for it. It was daft, but it made sense.

This point was made most forcibly, of course, when the recruit went to the Depot Stores to be issued with all his military kit. This would be his first meeting with it. It would be his first meeting, too, with an Army Colour Sergeant.

His full title would be Regimental Quartermaster Sergeant, or RQMS. So, at the same time, the recruit would make his first acquaintance with military mnemonics. The Armed Forces had a passion for them, and threw them around among themselves with mind-numbing abandon, complete with intervening full stops – O.R.Q.M.S., P.S.O., D.A.Q.M.G., R.S.M., C.I.G.S., and so on. The demise of the intervening full stop has done little to diminish its propensity for bafflement – KOYLI, KSLI, SHAFE.

They went a step further; they turned the mnemonic into a word in its own right. So the King's Own Scottish Borderers became, first, the K.O.S.B., and then the 'Kosbies'. The War Office Selection Board was known far and wide as 'Wosby'. The Unit Selection Board was 'Usby'. And every recruit probably knew already all about 'AWOL', certainly some of the more unco-operative ones – when they got caught.

The RQMS, then. You didn't make it to Colour Sergeant in five minutes; the chances were that he had over ten years' service to his credit, possibly more. That would have meant that he had taken part in the War, probably seen active service. By the time he had come to stand behind his capacious counter in the Quartermaster's Stores, he may have looked a trifle grizzled and overweight, but he had quite probably earned his medal ribbons – the 1939-45 star, the Defence Medal, the Italy Star, the North Africa Star, the Victory in Europe Medal, and so on. National Servicemen very often found themselves being trained by men with rows of ribbons on their chest. They had seen the real thing. Look at very senior officers today, and count up the ribbons. It won't take very long.

Not only might he have looked grizzled and overweight; he looked pretty forbidding too. He prided himself on the neatness of his Clothing Store (or rather 'Store Clothing'). Nothing so much as a mislaid Button, denim on the floor spoiled the ghostly absence of disarray. The arrival of a gaggle of callow recruits was a tiresome interruption to cherished routine which was to be got through as soon as possible, so that the Store could returned to its Trappist silence and parade order.

His storemen were well trained. They had had to do this scores of times. They stood at intervals along a counter as long as a railway platform, with piles of items of kit enough to prepare the recipients, it seemed, for a year on the Moon.

The RQMS stood with a huge list of items and names in his hand. The storemen had several forms at the ready. No recruit was to receive anything without first signing for it. He never had time to look at what he was signing. Vast, grid-like images swam before his eyes. As with the first-day documentation, any hesitation on his part as to where to sign was resolved by brown-stained fingers stabbed on to the paper. The by now inevitable blodgy biro was thrust forward. And the ritual began, led by the chanting of the RQMS:

'Bags kit, one – Shirts, angola, three – Vests, woollen, two – Drawers, woollen, two…'

As this was read out, the storemen awarded the recruit the item recited. As he did so, he too recited the same phrase. So it went like this:

'Belts, waist, one – '

'Belts, waist, one – '

'Pouches, basic, two – '

'Pouches, basic, two – '

'Trousers, denim, pairs, two – '

'Trousers, denim, pairs, two – '

They achieved such a machine-gun-like efficiency that the bemused recruit had to do almost nothing except move along the counter. He had already signed up for absolutely everything, including, so far as he knew, five years on Devil's Island. He simply made himself available as carrier. The storemen pushed things into his kitbag, thrust things under his belt, shoved things under his arms, draped things round his shoulders, stuffed things into his pockets, or balanced things on his head – 'Greatcoat, one' – 'Ties, khaki, one' – 'Pack, large, webbing, one'. . . .

The RQMS and his storemen did their job well. It was the first of many overwhelming experiences that the recruit had to deal with.

The next one was actually putting some of these garments on.

Boots were made of some kind of unyielding material which made them feel like clogs. Socks were of a prickliness which almost defied comparison. Cactus perhaps is the most accurate which comes to mind. Sweaters were hairy too. When, later, worn next to the skin for PE, they made everyone realise for the first time what the medieval saints had meant by mortification of the flesh. The denims were of one universal size, and clearly manufactured with a clear understanding of the extent of shrinkage which was to be inflicted by Army laundries. They would have been a perfect fit for a recruit six and a half feet tall, with a forty-inch waist and a fifty-inch chest.

Berets, on first wearing, stuck out all round like an upturned plate. Battledress blouses were shapeless and baggy. Trousers were scarcely Savile Row in their trimness. They had been awarded as a result of a casual, sizing-up glance by a storeman. Nobody had dared to make any mention to him of measurements. True, he did ask you what size you took in boots, but that was about all. (To be fair, there was a Depot tailor, who later made some alterations to battledress which removed the most outrageous anomalies.)

This, then, was the indispensable kit for the well-equipped soldier in Her Majesty's Forces in, roughly, the 1950s. One gesture to possible overseas service (and tropical overseas service at that) was the mysterious issue of lightweight pants, of a rather fetching shade of green. These were the famous Drawers jungle – three pairs of them. But, to young men, they were slightly preferable to the knee-length thigh-huggers which would have made their great-uncles wince at the anachronism – Drawers woollen. If Captain Oates had been wearing a pair of them, he might not have had to step outside for a moment.

The platoon – they were already getting used to the word – were now given time to put it all away in their lockers in some semblance of order. For those who, with loving mothers, had rarely had to keep even a satchel tidy, this represented quite a challenge.

But that was not the end of it. Far from it. Everyone now had to make sure that each piece of that kit could be identified with him. Soft items – Sweaters woollen, for instance, or Shorts, P.E., blue, pairs, two – had to have cotton labels sewn in, with the owner's name and Army number written on it. This maybe goes a long way to explain why no National Serviceman ever forgets his Army number. He had to spend nearly two whole days putting that number on every single item that he possessed.

When he had finished sewing it on to every soft piece of kit, he then had to write it or stamp it on every hard piece – Belts, webbing, or Pack, small, or Straps, webbing, even Bags, kit.

There were about twenty-four recruits in a platoon. There was one set of metal stamping kit. They soon learned the virtues of patience and teamwork. Fortunately, each man had been issued with several Needles, darning and a Housewife (work that one out), so they didn't have to queue to do the stitching – only go round cadging Germolene and plasters for pricked fingers and broken nails caused by trying to get the Buttons, denim through the material and splitting the button rings to fit them.

This normally took place on a Friday. Arrivals happened on a Thursday. Once they had staggered back to the barrack room with their kit, the recruits were allowed the rest of the weekend to get all this stamping done. Soldiering proper did not begin till the Monday morning. So they had plenty of time; most of them found that they needed it.

The Army authorities were still not finished with the business of kit. As the weeks went by, they would periodically set out to reassure themselves that no unit of this kit was lost, or allowed to become marred, dull, rough, untidy, creased, or in any way imperfect by their unearthly standards. An unavoidable, and memorable, part of basic training was the Kit Inspection.

Every item of kit (to repeat the phrase yet again) had now to be *taken out* of the locker and displayed on the recruit's bed. Neatly folded, of course, in regulation manner. Boots were to be laid out, not only clean, but laid over on their side, so as to show that the soles and heels and instep had been cleaned. Some regiments even insisted that the hobnails be polished. Some showed a preference for polished darning needles instead.

And every item had to be lined up. This meant that, if you squatted at the end of a row of beds and squinted down it, all the Mugs, china and and Pyjamas, cotton, pairs, two were in a straight line. Everything else too.

This could take hours to prepare – folding, polishing, ironing, lining up. Some weary, or worried, recruits, we were told, arranged all this the day before, and spent the night on the floor. Kit Inspection.

CHAPTER 10
Pregnant Ducks

So far so good: the recruit had found his way to the barracks; he had learned the lay-out of his barrack room; he had got to know what a member of the Permanent Staff looked like; he had survived his first foray into the 'Ablutions'; he had met the rest of the platoon; he had signed for, and jammed into his locker, the mountain of unfamiliar kit with which he had been issued; and he had discovered that one did not address corporals and sergeants as 'Sir'. The next step was to make the acquaintance of the more lofty Depot dignitaries – who *did* have to be addressed as 'Sir'.

The first was the RSM – a further set of initials which became engraved more indelibly than the others on his memory. Why? Because they stood for 'Regimental Sergeant-Major'.

The Sergeant-Major is perhaps the second-best-known cliché about the Army (the first is 'square-bashing', and the third is 'bull' – both of which will be dealt with in this book at a later stage). He is, according to legend, large, looming, and loud. Mostly true; one very rarely saw small RSM's. Since he was in charge of Depot discipline (under the Adjutant, usually a captain, sometimes a major), he had to be pretty fearsome; that's what he was there for. Loud too – he had to issue many parade-ground commands. It was also his duty to march offenders into the CO's office for trial (and usually punishment), which he did at the top of his voice.

He was a warrant officer; he held the Queen's warrant, just as an officer held the Queen's commission. There were two classes, I and II. A depot could have several WO IIs – usually known as Company Sergeant Majors, and addressed as 'Sergeant-Major' – or, as usage progressed, as 'Sarn't-Major', even 'Sah-Major'. You could have a WO II in charge of, say, the Training Company (the recruits), or of Depot P.E., or Depot transport, or whatever. They wore a crown on their sleeve. But there was normally only one WO I – whose sleeve bore the royal coat of arms. There was only one Regimental Sergeant-Major – thank God.

He was not only entitled to be addressed as 'Sir'; he was entitled to carry a pace-stick, as an officer carried a baton, and, on formal parades, to wear a sword. Even officers were required to use the prefix 'Mr' when addressing him. Since any Army (or any other armed service) is based on discipline and the sanctity of orders, the man responsible for maintaining that discipline carried a big burden. He was probably the one whose influence was most widely felt. His was probably the most notorious rank, the one the general public was best aware of. Nine recruits out of ten entered the Army prepared to be scared of the RSM; nine out of ten RSMs did not disappoint them. Whichever way you looked at it, the RSM was a pretty big wheel.

It was the RSM, then, who marshalled the platoon into a convenient hut, to be harangued by the Commanding Officer. Scalding glares. Nervy fingering of his pace-stick. Sudden bawlings. 'Silence!' 'Room? Rooooooom – SHUN!' That sort of thing.

Recruits were told to sit down, and 'smoke if you wish'. So this was to be the friendly bit. To show that the Army was really on their side.

Surprisingly, many did – smoke. Another obvious difference between 1948 and 2012. Soldiers smoked. It was only about a decade after the War, less if you were one of the early intakes. The habit was by this time in the nation's bloodstream. Society may be more enlightened now, and more aware of the dangers of tobacco, but stress can make one forget common sense in the face of the greater need to survive with nerves intact. Ask veterans of Iraq or Afghanistan.

So the smokers sat back and puffed and looked questioningly at each other, and wondered what the CO was going to say.

The Depot Commanding Officer, to most of the Depot's inmates, was a distant figure of legendary authority, with mystical powers of omniscience, and a Jehovah-like capacity for detecting backsliding. Worse than Jehovah – no slaughtered lamb could mitigate his inevitable and merciless punishment. Like Jehovah, too, one very rarely actually saw him. The one time his presence could be guaranteed was when he gave the new intake his Opening Address. It was not unknown for him to put on blues – his Number One uniform – to do this. His contribution, presumably, to the calculated informality of the occasion – the sitting down, berets off, 'smoke if you wish', and so on.

The Address itself took about five minutes, if that: he daresaid that they would all be finding the Army pretty strange right then, but they were not to worry, because they would all get used to things pretty quickly, especially if they knuckled down to it, worked hard, and did as they were told. Take their Army uniforms – unfamiliar and ill-fitting. At that moment, they all looked like pregnant ducks. (Pause for laughter.) But they would soon get the hang of things. They were going to be given training in P.E. and drill and the basic military weapons, in order to get them to the highest possible standard of military fitness. Their instructors were first-class men who knew their job and whose one aim was to turn them into efficient soldiers. Indeed, all the Depot staff were there to help them, and they were not to hesitate to turn to any of them if they were in trouble. They were in the Army for the next two years, whether they liked it or not, and it was up to each of them to make the most of it. He wished them the best of luck.

The RSM extinguished the relaxed atmosphere in a flash:

'Room! Rooooooom – shun!' Followed by a twitch of the pace stick and a salute which made even the CO wince. And that was that.

Well, not quite.

Hastily-crushed cigarettes had hardly been slid back into Woodbines packets when the RSM went into his routine again – 'Room! Roooooom – SHUN!'

The new arrival wore ordinary battledress – not blues. But he too was a major. (For all his awesome reputation, the CO was only a major.) He put down his hat, slid his thumbs under the chest flaps of his battledress blouse (oddly feminine nomenclature for a piece of fighting uniform), and invited the gathering to 'smoke if you wish'.

He told the platoon that he was the man in charge of their training – the Training Company Commander. That fitted with what the knowledgeable ones already knew, and what the ignorant ones soon found out. The smallest unit in an army (a British army, at any rate), was a section. Two or three sections made a platoon, about twenty-odd. Three or four platoons constituted a company. In this case it was only two platoons in the company – the new arrivals and the 'veterans' of the senior intake, with six weeks of soldiering already under their belts. No doubt bigger Depots would have had three or four training platoons, or even more.

Three or four companies went to make up a battalion. There would also be a 'Headquarter Company', which held the cooks, batmen, clerks, drivers, and so on; the actual fighting would be done by the four companies. The whole force was commanded by a lieutenant-colonel. About 900-1000 men. This was the unit which, full of trained men, represented the regiment on active service – usually referred to simply as 'the battalion'. A regiment could have more than one of these 'battalions' serving abroad somewhere.

That was as far as the average recruit's knowledge usually went, or needed to go. Battalions made up brigades, and brigades divisions, commanded by brigadiers and major-generals respectively. Ninety-nine soldiers out of a hundred could count on one hand the number of brigadiers and major-generals they met during their service. Dammit, it was an event if they saw the Commanding Officer of their Training Company.

This gentleman, having created the desired atmosphere of relaxation, surmised that the platoon was probably finding the Army pretty strange right then, but they were not to worry. They would all get used to things pretty quickly, especially if they knuckled down to it, worked hard, and did as they were told. Take their Army uniforms – unfamiliar and ill-fitting. At that moment, they all looked like pregnant ducks. (Pause for polite laughter.) But they would soon get the hang of things. They were going to be given training in P.E. and drill and the basic military weapons . . . . and it was up to each of them to make the most of it. He wished them the best of luck.

The RSM did his 'Room shun' routine, and the hapless cigarettes were stubbed out again.

The Training Company Commander was followed by a much younger man, with only one pip on his shoulder. He jumped slightly when the RSM, having bawled 'Room – shun', flung up another flawless salute, but had the presence of mind to return it. He placed his shiny new baton on the desk, stood back, and leapt forward again just in time to prevent it rolling off.

The chances were that he too was a National Serviceman, fresh from four months' officer training. He had probably been in the Army himself only about nine or ten months.

After graciously inviting those present to – guess what – he said that, as their Training Platoon Commander, he thought it was appropriate that he should say a few words to them all, by way of introducing himself, and of letting them know what was in store for them in the coming twelve weeks.

They were – er – probably finding their uniforms pretty uncomfortable, and they certainly looked like a lot of – er – pregnant ducks. . . . training in the basic military weapons. . . . first-class men. . . . whether they liked it or not. . . . the best of luck.

And that really was that. The last 'Room – shun!'. Putting the cigarette out of its misery. And back to the sewing and writing and stamping – for hours.

What they probably took away with them was the 'pregnant duck' joke. If indeed it was a joke. To be fair, it was not entirely inapt; the uniforms did look awful on most of them, and did nothing for their figures or their posture.

Funny or not, it was a good example of the words and phrases that came to figure in a recruit's life for the coming three months. They were often part of an NCO's armoury of invective, part of the game, part of the business of getting on with it, long after it had had all the possible humour squeezed out of it.

'Bleedn' Christ! – you look like a twisted sick report' was not all that funny the *first* time, never mind all the others. The exhortation by a parade-ground sergeant that a drill movement should be smart and crisp 'like a violin string goin' twang!' was not even particularly apt, let alone funny. It just became part of life.

One style of invective that appealed to many NCO's was the imputation that the squad was made up of homosexuals – 'mincin' along there like a bunch of queers on 'olidy'. It sounds particularly offensive in these days of political correctness, but it did not then; it was just a feeble joke, intended really to imply not that the squad in question was homosexual to a man, but that they were weak, ineffective, effete, soft, no use as soldiers, and the use of something suggesting unmanliness helped this comparison.

It was part of the familiar technique of hyperbole. The most famous sergeant-major in the Army – or so the tabloid press claimed – used to say, time and again, 'Never seen anything like it in all me life!' He was even put in a feature film using this line.

Then there were the gems of moralising which were drummed into a recruit's head: completing a smart drill movement meant 'picking your feet up nine inches and driving it in twelve'; a sentry who went to sleep was 'endangering the lives of his comrades' (well, he was); 'drill teaches a soldier self-respect and pride in the uniform he wears' (it does actually); 'leave was a privilege, not an entitlement'. Any ex-national serviceman has a whole portfolio of these remarks stored away in his memory as immovably as the gold is stored in Fort Knox.

Finally, there were the constantly-used single words or phrases: 'get a grip'; 'fall in'; 'fall out'; 'leave pass'; 'fatigues' – dozens of them, which are burned into a recruit's psyche.

One in particular was 'Barrack Room Duties'.

When the platoon returned from their pep talks, they found, pinned to the wall, a list of the different tasks each of them had to perform in order to maintain their room to the standard of cleanliness and order apparently required by the Depot authorities. And perform every single working day. (The Army did normally recognise the Sabbath as a day apart; they could be oddly Victorian sometimes. It was probably a relic of so many Victorian values that hung over from the nineteenth century.)

Most of them made sense. One member would have to sweep those parts of the floor which were not 'covered' by the individual bed-spaces – say, round the stove. Another had to dust the lampshades. A third had to clean the window-sills. No dust was allowed to settle on the surface of the fire buckets (or rather 'Buckets, fire, hand'). One poor devil had to clean the wash-basins, and another even poorer devil had to get to work with the brush and mop on the lavatory pans. These duties were regularly swapped around, so nobody could complain of discrimination or unfairness. Difficult to complain about.

One or two, though, were preposterous. One involved arranging the brooms around the stove, with the handles resting on the top of it, and the heads reaching outwards like the points of the compass. And, at the end of it all, another poor devil had to arm himself with a razor blade and scrape the accumulated dirt off the handles of the brooms. It could end up, after several weeks and over-zealous broom-scrapers, with truly anorexic handles as slender as the models in *Vogue*.

On this topic, rumour and tall story abounded. Anecdotes about the polishing of the floorboards till they shone. More anecdotes about one barracks where the central floorboard had to be done out in a different colour from the others, and there must be no careless spreading of the wrong colour over the cracks. And everybody has heard the story about whitewashing the coal. Rather like the case of the Abominable Snowman: everybody knows about it but nobody has actually seen it.

By the end of their first weekend, the platoon had been made aware of the innumerable things that were expected of them, and had it drummed into their heads what dire punishments awaited them if they fell short.

What could in fact happen to them? They could be confined to barracks for a certain time. Not much of a deterrent, because none of them was allowed out at all until he had satisfied the authorities that he could wear his uniform to the required standard of smartness; in other words, to show that he no longer looked like a pregnant duck. It might take three or four weeks.

They could have their pay stopped if they damaged a piece of equipment or furniture, or lost an item of equipment – which also made sense. They could be given extra duties – usually 'fatigues' of one kind or another. Like scraping fat out of the huge cooking pans in the kitchen, or delivering coal to the Married Quarters (known, for some odd reason of quaint respectability, as 'Married Families' – it wouldn't be so accurate today).

Serious offences could land a miscreant in the guardroom for so many days. Worse crimes could put him in the Army prison at Colchester.

What usually got him in trouble was yet another of those evocative words that the Army treasured, perhaps above all others, and which was used ubiquitously: 'Idle.'

It meant laziness, of course. So, if a soldier was not performing his foot drill with enough urgency to satisfy his drill sergeant, he could be called 'idle'. Which he was. If he was not running fast enough round the gym, he was 'idle'. Again, fair enough.

But that was only the start. If a boot was not polished enough, it was 'idle'; if a piece of webbing had gaps in its blanco covering, it was 'idle'; if a belt had carelessly-left, minute spots of blanco marring the shine of its brass fittings, it was 'idle'. You could have idle gaiters, idle small packs, large packs, ammunition pouches, rifle slings, rifle barrels, laces (which were twisted instead of flat). 'Idle' anything in fact. If you did not slap your rifle hard enough in drill, *you* were idle. In theory, a whole damned platoon could be idle.

Idleness merited condign punishment. But this was not the Middle Ages; the Army had to punish you legally. None of the 'off-with-his-head' attitude. There was an Act of Parliament which specified a terrifyingly long list of offences which could carry a bewildering variety of punishments. It was called, very succinctly and appropriately, the Army Act.

The trouble was that the lawyers who drew up its terms could not possibly foresee every conceivable offence which a hamfisted recruit might commit. The sharpest legal eagle could not have provided for an 'idle belt brass'. So the experts came up with a final 'offence' which took in everything: 'conduct to the prejudice of good order and military discipline'. That got 'em.

Not even an idle Needles, darning was outside the law.

CHAPTER 11
'Toon! Tooooon – shun!

It was remarked in Chapter Ten that the Regimental Sergeant-Major was the second-most-common cliché about the Army. The commonest of all, the most quoted, the most hackneyed, the one which provoked the greatest laughter among those who had not the faintest idea what they were talking about, was drill – what the ignoramuses loved to call 'square-bashing'.

It was what every national serviceman about to enter the Armed Forces expected to be doing for a large slice of his day. He knew it was about marching, and stamping feet, and loud commands, and fierce sergeants and sergeant-majors and staff sergeants and petty officers. He found very soon that it was also about hard work and cold mornings and freezing fingers and aching muscles and stiff necks. He noticed that it was what he got teased about by his family and so-called friends before he began, and also when he was able to get home on leave. It was what comedians and script-writers and film directors concentrated on. It was a pain. It was the oldest joke in the book.

There was certainly a great deal of it. It was inescapable. Its ubiquity and total pervasiveness were to make it an indelible memory of his National Service. It did not make it any more palatable.

Just as a small boy finds it difficult to accept the necessity for etiquette and good manners and opening doors for girls, so a recruit found it difficult to appreciate the need for all this endless stamping and marching and wheeling and turning. What did it have to do with fighting? What was the point of being parade-ground soldiers or sailors or airmen? When had a perfect parade ever won a war?

The authorities had an answer for that. A war was won by the side which was, among other things, the best organised and the most purposeful. That was achieved by discipline and hard work, and that in turn was achieved by everyone doing what he was told – without question. Most people are not used to being ordered about. It could begin in the cradle; there are parents who pride themselves on the fact that they never say 'no' to their infants. Teachers will tell you that children don't listen to what they are being taught. People don't read bye-laws or small print or instructions on packets. They don't park in the right places or fill in forms correctly. Some vaunt what they like to think is their sense of independence, but then the chances are that other people will not die as a result of this 'independence'. It is not quite like that in the Services.

If an organisation depends totally on the sanctity of command – like the Army and the Navy and the Air Force – then a system has to be devised to ensure that people *do* listen to instructions – and carry them out – at once. What they came up with was drill.

Drill was designed – and here I quote from the Drill Manual ('all arms') issued by the War Office in 1951, and published by HM Stationery Office ('price 2s. 6d' – 12½p.) – 'to develop in the individual soldier that sense of instinctive obedience which will assist him at all times to carry out his orders. That the foundation of discipline in battle is based on drill has been proved again and again.'

And nobody who has not been in battle has the right to refute that. So listen to what the book has to say:

'Good drill, well rehearsed, closely supervised, and demanding the highest precision is an exercise in obedience and alertness. It sets the standard for the execution of any duty, both for the individual and the unit, and builds up that sense of confidence between commander and subordinate which is so essential in battle.

'Good drill and a high standard are not learnt on the barrack square merely to be discarded in everyday life except for ceremonial occasions. It is the constant duty of those in command to insist on the standard they know to be right both on and off parade and in all circumstances. Once an idle action or bad turnout is allowed to pass, whether during the recruit stage or later, the standard is lowered and further bad habits will follow.'

Well, that's what it says.

Of course, the NS recruit did not see it like that. He was not in a position to see it like that. He couldn't care less about the Army's side of it; he was too busy doing his best to survive his own side of it. He didn't want to be in the bloody Army in the first place. All he saw (and felt) was a lot of work, a lot of shouting, a lot of repetition, and devilish high standards of dress expected at all times – with unavoidable, tiresome, unpleasant, and undignified punishments if they were not met.

All that effort devoted to senseless exercises of pettifogging precision, all that attention lavished on trivial detail, all those silly demands which would not impose on your average chimpanzee.

Well, they were all in for a surprise, several surprises in fact.

The first was the realisation that drill was not as easy as it looked, or as it sounded when you glanced it from a comfortable distance. Take the simple business of the position of attention.

Everyone knows, or thinks they know, that it means standing up straight. Well, anybody can do that.

No, they can't – not the way the Army meant it. Listen to the book again:

'Heels together and in line; feet turned out to an angle of 30 degrees; knees braced; body erect and with the weight balanced evenly between the ball of the feet and the heels; shoulders down and back (so as to bring the chest to a normal position without straining or stiffening), level, and square to the front; arms hanging straight from the shoulders, elbows close to the sides, wrists straight, hands closed (not clenched), backs of the fingers close to the thighs, thumbs straight and to the front, close to the forefinger and just behind the seam of the trousers; head up, neck feeling the collar, eyes open, steady and looking their own height.'

Over twenty things to get right. All at the same time. It took practice to get any one of them right, but to synchronise them – countless times – on demand. You didn't achieve that without alertness and precision, and that meant concentration – it was *not* as easy as falling off a log.

The irony was that, the more they concentrated, the more tiring it became. They made the beginner's mistake of trying too hard, as everyone does. After a while, muscles began to ache. If they had been able to look at the drill book, they would have noticed that the position of attention was not designed to produce the maximum of discomfort – on the contrary.

Look at the words. 'Feet turned out to an angle of 30 degrees' – much more natural than feet close together. 'The weight evenly balanced between the ball of the feet and the heels' – the broader the base the better the stability. 'Shoulders down and back (so as to bring the chest to a normal position without straining or stiffening' – it actually says *'without straining or stiffening'*. 'Arms hanging straight from the shoulders' – 'hanging', not thrusting. 'Hands closed (*not clenched*)'. 'Eyes… looking their own height' – which seems pretty natural.

And that was only the beginning. They were learning the position of attention. It was hard enough just being there. Now they had to learn the business of *getting* there.

How did they get there? From the position of 'at ease'. That took some learning too. What did the book say? '… the feet are about 12 inches apart'. The arms are 'behind the back, keeping them straight' … with 'the back of the right hand in the palm of the left, thumbs crossed, fingers and thumbs straight and pointing towards the ground', and so on. Like everything else, all right when you have learned it, but it has to be learned.

So, one would have thought, once you had learned the position of 'at ease' and the position of 'attention', it would be a simple matter to transfer from the one to the other.

Not a bit of it.

The book was ahead again. It has sections labelled 'Common Faults'. These were the 'common faults' of the 'attention' position:

'i) A strained and exaggerated position, causing breathing to be restricted.

 Unsteadiness and movement of the eyes.

 Feet and body not square to the front, heels not closed.

 Arms slightly bent and creeping forward.

 Backs of the hands to the front, thereby opening the shoulder blades and constricting the chest.

 Wrists crooked and strained, knuckle of the forefinger projecting below the other fingers.'

That was what it said in the book. What happened in real practice could be even worse. In order to get from the 'at ease' position to 'attention', you obviously had to move your left foot and place it beside the right (taking care of course to leave the feet at an angle of 30 degrees); you moved your hands from behind your back to your sides (remembering to have the arms straight, your shoulders level and square to the front, your neck against your collar, your thumbs facing forward and just behind the seam of the trousers, your fingers closed (but not clenched) and your eyes open, steady, and looking your own height.

Firstly, the heels did not arrive at their destination together; the result was a sort of staccato clatter. Many did not arrive at all, because they had travelled too far and crashed down against the inside of the other heel, causing bruising and removing layers of carefully-applied boot polish. Some did not travel far enough, and left the poor owner at a position of 'half at ease'. Arms were pushed too far down, so that the owners had to push out their stomachs to compensate, which, as a result of the bagginess of the new battledress, caused to appear some very maternal outlines. Arms flailed. Hands, fingers, and thumbs landed all over the place. Desperate attempts to check that everything was in order resulted in a lot of leaning and peering.

It needs little imagination to work out the sort of remarks the drill sergeant or corporal would make about all this.

So far, in his drill training, the recruit had learned only to move his left foot – from the 'at ease' to 'attention'. And look at the trouble he was in.

So 'your average chimpanzee' soon dropped out of the equation. It wasn't a doddle after all.

Lying in wait for them was a vast repertoire of movements which the book had reduced to a series of precise and highly-detailed actions: starting to march, coming to a halt; turning, to the left, to the right, and right round; turning when you were still; turning when you were marching; wheeling, to the left and to the right; forming up in twos and forming up in threes; standing in ranks close together ('close order') and further apart ('open order'); marching in quick time, marching in slow time; switching from quick to slow time, and vice-versa. The show-piece was 'advance in review order'. That came at the end, when you were practising for the passing-out parade.

As with so many unwelcome jobs that one is faced with, there was, in the end, some satisfaction to be derived from getting it right, and it was so with drill – though one didn't like admitting it.

Curiously, the book recognised that drill instructors had responsibilities too. On page 112, it emphasised the paramount importance of the instructor setting an example in both dress and behaviour, and warned that 'bad language will not be tolerated'.

CHAPTER 12
Idle Belts

The word 'bull' became so much a permanent part of a recruit's life – and still an inescapable part, later, of a trained soldier's life as well – that it needed a great effort of the imagination to think of a time when they were not acquainted with it. It was as if 'in the beginning was the Word, and the Word was Bull'. Not only that; they would have found it almost unbelievable that everybody else did not know what it was. It would have been like asking a nursing mother what was meant by the word 'nappy'.

For the benefit of the few ignorant, benighted souls who may remain out there in the unreal world, 'bull' was to do with the care of a soldier's kit. In fact, despite what servicemen may think, the universe has *not* always known about it, because the New Shorter Oxford English Dictionary informs us that its origin goes back only to the mid-twentieth century.

Did this take in the Second World War – 1939-1945? Or was the reference being even more precise? National Service began with the National Service Act of 1948; was the word 'bull' coined by national servicemen? They were the ones who suffered most notoriously from it, and the word 'bull' had other associations – implying ideas like trivial, nonsensical, pettifogging, excessive, and so on. So was it some articulate sufferer who, very early on in National Service, transferred the epithet to cover what everybody in the Services came to understand by it?

The dictionary picked it up: as a noun, it meant 'unnecessary routine tasks or ceremonial', or 'pointlessly excessive discipline'; as a verb, it meant to 'polish (equipment, etc.) in order to meet excessive standards of neatness'.

Note, not 'multifarious routine tasks' but 'unnecessary routine tasks'; not 'stern discipline' but 'pointlessly excessive discipline'; not 'severe standards of neatness' but 'excessive standards of neatness'. So the dictionary had homed in on the feature of kit-cleaning which had thrust itself on the daily life, and daily thinking, of the recruit: it was not the cleaning they found objectionable; it was the 'excessive' part of it, the 'pointless' part of it.

Whole chapters, of course, could be written to debate exactly when 'multifarious' became 'unnecessary', when 'severe' standards of neatness became 'excessive'. No doubt every military establishment had its own standards which it took pride in enforcing, and countless stories were swapped in the barrack room about the outrageous excesses perpetrated by the barracks up the road or the regiment in the next county, or the Guards, or the Marines, or whatever.

It has to be an immovable chapter in any account of a national serviceman's life because its impact was such a shock. A regular soldier or sailor or airman had at least *chosen* to enlist; he had made his bed, and was expected therefore to lie on it without too much complaint. But a national serviceman had not chosen it, and he did not like the bed the Services had told him to lie on, for two whole years – not very long when you are, say, sixty, but an awful lot when you are eighteen.

As has already been explained, there were those who had led such a sheltered or disorganised life that even modest standards of smartness and self-organisation would have come as a seismic shock. But even those who could fairly claim that they kept themselves and their possessions smart and clean were to be taken aback, discomfited, amazed, staggered by the standards they were called upon to meet.

So Service bulling became the stuff of complaint, recrimination, anecdote, and legend. Like the bad film which is so bad that, in the process of time and after many viewings, it becomes good, the bulling transcended disbelief and dismay and became a joke. Every unit had their own story about their own local 'excess' or their own local martinet who seemed to think of nothing else but piddling detail, and enforcing it. Perversely they almost took pride in it.

It was the cross which united all national servicemen; everybody, absolutely everybody, was affected. Who knows? Perhaps some psychologist at Armed Forces Medical Head-quarters had dreamed it up as a means of creating the unity which comes from joint suffering.

More soberly, the manual already quoted in Chapter Eleven was alive to the value of creating high standards, and maintaining them: 'Once an idle action or bad turnout is allowed to pass, whether during the recruit stage or later, the standard is lowered and further bad habits will follow.' Unarguable; to say that you disagreed was like claiming that you disapproved of virtue.

Note the use of the word 'idle'. Barracks authorities and NCOs descended rapaciously upon this humble little adjective, and put it to work in a thousand capacities (again, see Chapter Eleven). It became the dray-horse which pulled the great and unstoppable cart of service discipline. Anything unacceptable was 'idle' – behaviour, marching, drill movements, scruffy boots, bad blanco, dull belt brasses, top kit (more later), insides of lockers, rifle barrels – they were all 'idle'.

A great deal of time, therefore, had to be spent making sure that clothes, equipment, lockers, and anything else for which the recruit was responsible was *not* 'idle'. Hence, bulling. It produced dirty hands, bent backs, sweat-soaked foreheads, frustration, bafflement, worry, and despair. Fortunately, it also produced inventiveness, co-operation, and not a little satisfaction, even at times pride. So perhaps that psychologist was on to something after all.

To take the negative side first. Let us start with boots. Boots had to be polished – OK. But it was not as simple as that. To be fair, the everyday boots, for lessons, lectures, fatigues, marching, firing on the range, and everything else, did not attract much of an eagle eye; they were expected to be clean, little more. But the parade boots – the second pair – they were the ones in which you had to be able to see your face.

Just to make the challenge interesting, the boots, when they first reached you, were covered with countless little pimples, all of which had to be removed before one could begin to produce a shine on smooth leather. Incidentally, the truth about why they were called 'ammunition boots' is rather more prosaic than the speculations offered in Chapter Nine. Apparently, for decades the Army's boots were produced at Woolwich Arsenal, which was the home of military ordnance – guns, bullets, and so on – and so were known as 'ammunition' boots. QED.

Even if the recruits had known the truth about their boots' origins, it would not have been any help. And they would have gnashed their teeth in fury if they had known what is available today: there are websites on the internet which offer to 'bull' pairs of boots to the required standard. All you have to do is send them £160, and the goods are delivered in perfect order (well, that's what the websites say).

The recruits – poor souls – were left to get on with it – all of it. Their cap badge had to shine like a second sun. Brasses – the fitments on belts and webbing – had to dazzle. Webbing itself – belts and straps – had to display a perfect surface, achieved by a meticulous application of countless layers of blanco – the paste type (a slightly sickly green) or the powder-mixed-with-water type (usually a dirty sand colour). Gaiters needed blanco too. So did the rifle sling. It was a mercy that by the time most national servicemen joined up, the Army had evolved a type of button which did not require polishing – which made one wonder why their boffins didn't come up with similar formulas for other items. But no – much too logical.

And mere cleanliness and shine were not enough. The ammunition pouches and the two packs ('Packs large' and 'Packs small') had to be lined with carefully-tailored pieces of stiff cardboard so that they gave a geometric boxed effect. The procedure was indeed known far and wide as 'boxing' kit. All these items, moreover, were to be arranged in a tightly-prescribed pattern on top of the locker, so that every possible brass was on view for an eagle-eyed inspecting officer or NCO to be dissatisfied with. It was known, not surprisingly, as 'top kit'.

If indeed the inspecting officer was not satisfied with a man's top kit, the customary way of indicating this dissatisfaction was, with a dramatic gesture of the arm, to sweep the entire collection on to the floor. The owner, who was standing by the foot of his bed and therefore could not see what was going on behind him, knew perfectly what was happening by the sound. He knew too that that sound meant the end of his chances of getting away at Saturday lunchtime for a prompt weekend pass, because he would be 'bulling' his 'top kit' yet again before showing it to the duty officer – in the hope maybe of catching a mid-afternoon train.

Battledress came in for the bull treatment too: creases had to be razor-sharp and in the right places, to the centimetre. Other kit on display had to be 'correctly' folded. Greatcoats were impossible to press, but they had to be folded and put on show – of course – in the 'correct' way. Otherwise they would be deemed 'idle'.

About the only items of kit that were not 'bulled' were the tin hat and the knife, fork, and spoon – and the china mug. Even the Army recognised that hygiene would not be helped by eating utensils being blancoed or plastered with Kiwi polish, and they had clearly given up on the tin hats.

Rifles were not as a rule kept in barrack rooms, for obvious reasons of security, but during the period when the recruit was issued with them (for training during the day), they were his responsibility, and think of all the bits and pieces that were set into, bolted to, clipped on to, slid into, or otherwise attached to, a Lee-Enfield rifle.

It is worth noting that nothing was supplied for this bulling to be done; a recruit had to get it all in the NAAFI shop, which was a universal component of any military depot. (NAAFI stood for 'Navy, Army, and Air Forces Institute' – a sort of general welfare organisation.) But it was not given away; everything – polish, dusters, everything – had to come out of a recruit's weekly pay of £1.40.

With so many items to be kept clean, and so many young men (often national servicemen themselves, with a mere six months' service behind them) with a stripe or two on their sleeve and a figure to cut, it is hardly surprising that there was plenty of scope for finicky fault-finding – which was another small cross that the recruit had to bear.

But the situation called forth inventiveness too, and teamwork. For example, one man would discover that he had a knack with boots, another with cap badges, a third with pressing uniform. Knowledge was exchanged, advice was offered (and thankfully taken), help was given.

Gradually, as the twelve weeks advanced, the recruits developed expertise, experience, and a sense of perspective. There were, of course, the worriers who could, and often did, devote five or six frantic hours every evening to bulling kit. At the other extreme, there were those worldly loafers who tried, and often succeeded, in getting away with the very minimum. But the majority got by with a fair amount of effort – and perhaps a little optimism and luck.

Did it do any good in the long run or was it all waste? No doubt there were those who, as soon as they were demobbed, slipped back into their former slovenliness. But they were all young – only 18 to 21 – and impressionable; many often found habits ingrained by the Forces hard to break. Ever afterwards they would not leave the house wearing dirty shoes; they would not attend a formal function with trousers that badly needed pressing.

CHAPTER 13
Making a Noise

National Servicemen, most of them, were only eighteen years old – plus those who joined three years late after their university courses. A small minority joined even later, because they had embarked on post-graduate study. Indeed a still smaller minority attempted to secure places on so many consecutive degree courses that success would have taken them beyond the age of twenty-six, the cut-off age for NS conscription. No doubt a few of them made it. (There were some too who chose to go down the mines for two years – which some might say is an odd preference.)

However, they were all young, that is the point. Young, and malleable. More to the point, they were all likely anyway to be influenced by an institution and its regulations under whose sway they spent every waking minute (and every sleeping minute too). The Army, or the Navy, or the Air Force, simply took over, and had regulations for every facet and feature of a recruit's life. (Rumour had it that they even concocted a set of regulations for the correct position of sleeping.)

As already observed, one of the things that first took the recruit aback was noise – verbal commands were not merely loud; they were volcanic. And delivered often within inches of the face. But such was the pervasive influence of service life that recruits came, if not to like it, at any rate to tolerate it.

They could even see the sense of certain elements: for instance, if a sergeant was on a parade-ground, with his recruits marching sixty or seventy yards away from him, he had to make sure that his voice carried to them; if a sergeant-major was in charge of a big parade with hundreds of soldiers spread out over an area approaching an acre, he needed to have a strong voice, and he needed to be able to project it.

But that was only the beginning: he had been subjected to the end-of-the-world charade of the duty corporal getting him up in the morning (see Chapter Eight); he had been told countless times to 'pick your foot up nine inches and drive it in twelve'; the dawn bugle also had a Last-Trump dimension to it.

The wilting recruit was forced to live in a world of bawling, banging, and stamping. (Perhaps, for once, a cliché was not so far from the truth – 'square-bashing'.) But such is the resilience of the human frame and psyche, and such is the impressionability of the young, that he came to accept it. So when he moved from foot drill to rifle drill, it came as no surprise to be told that he was expected to make a noise with that too.

This obsession with noise showed itself in the very verbiage of the training pamphlet. He was never told to 'move' or 'place' something; he had to 'drive' it, 'strike' it, 'force' it. Perhaps this went back to one of the oldest military maxims in any book: if you want to unnerve the enemy, make a whacking great big noise. It went back still further to biological origins: lions don't roar just to clear their throat.

Be that as it may, the training book had about 28 pages devoted to foot drill, plus a further nine concerned with saluting. When it came to rifle drill, the book came up with another twenty-odd, and a postscript of four more on how to handle the rifle at public funerals.

Perhaps fortunately, the average NS recruit was unlikely to be called upon to line the Mall for the cortège of a prince of the realm, but he still had over twenty pages of skills and movements to master in the everyday handling of 'the soldier's best friend'.

As with foot drill, the explanations and comments which follow may go some way towards dispelling the legend that 'square-bashing' is some kind of joke that does little else but provide amusement for the general public. The implication is that it is no *use*; it just gives the Army something to make recruits do; it makes few demands on the intelligence. Taken all round, the whole thing is pretty daft.

Well, let us consider what is involved – or rather what *was* involved; the old Lee-Enfield ·303 rifle which was the bane of a national serviceman's life has long since been superseded.

It weighed nine pounds for a start. It had bolt-handles and magazines and knobs and buckles and back-sights and fore-sights which protruded all over the place, and it was the most awkward shape to move about one's person. Move, moreover, using only the hands and arms, and without moving the body or the head. The eyes throughout had to remain staring fixedly ahead.

By way of example, let us take the pamphlet's instructions on the correct procedure for moving the rifle from the 'Order' (when the weapon is at the soldier's right side, with the butt resting on the ground beside his right boot) to the 'Slope' (by which time it has been moved so that it rests on the soldier's left shoulder, with his left hand holding its butt and his right hand back at his side – 'with the thumbs down the seam of the trousers').

'The slope from the order.

'1. "Slope arms – one" – Throw the rifle straight up the right side with a vigorous flick of the wrist, keeping the elbow still, and release it before the right hand reaches the level of the waist belt jerking the right arm straight again; at the same time move the left arm across the body and catch the rifle just below the upper sling swivel, hand in line with the right armpit, knocking the rifle back into the right shoulder; strike the rifle with the palm of the hand, closing the fingers and thumb of the left hand round the rifle, and as the left hand strikes the rifle catch the butt with the fingers and thumb of the right hand.

'*Note* – The fingers and thumb of the right hand will be in the same position as at attention, but will hold the butt so that the forefinger is about in line with the knuckle of the butt, rifle perpendicular with the magazine to the front.

'2. "Squad – two" – Force the rifle across the body so that the muzzle passes just in front of the face; as soon as the muzzle has passed the face and the left hand is about in line with the left breast pocket, let go of the rifle with the left hand and drop the hand so that the elbow is against the side (as at attention), forearm parallel to the ground and at right angles to the body, wrist straight; at the same time move the fingers and thumb of the right hand round the rifle and drive the butt into the heel of the left hand just before the magazine touches the left shoulder; close the fingers and thumb of the left hand round the butt so that the thumb is round the toe of the butt and about one inch above the butt plate and the fingers, from the centre knuckles to the tips are together on top of the butt, and point towards the muzzle.

'*Note* – The magazine will now point to the left and be flat on the shoulder just below the collar bone.

'3. "Squad – three" – Cut the right hand the nearest way to the position of attention; keep the wrist stiff and curl up the fingers on the downward travel; keep the rifle still.'

Everything all right so far?

So far we have mentioned only the procedure for getting from the 'Order' to the 'Slope'. Not surprisingly, the Army had a prescribed method for getting from the 'Slope' to the 'Order'. In fact, it should come as no surprise to the reader by now to discover that the Army (and the Navy and Air Force) had a prescribed method for doing practically everything.

What else was there to do with the rifle? (Apart of course from the business of shooting with it – that comes later.)

Quite a lot. You had to 'Present' it for a start. That was the movement for paying an official compliment – to high-powered visitors, royalty, the regimental colours, and so on. The training pamphlet has nearly an entire page of details for this.

Not only that; it had a good half-page detailing what it called 'common faults': 'making a circular movement with the right arm and letting the the right elbow leave the body'; 'not gripping the rifle with the fingers of the right hand round the butt'; 'moving the butt to the right to meet the right hand'. And that was only the first movement; there were two other movements in the whole manoeuvre, each of which also carried caveats about 'common faults'.

The recruit did not of course have to read all these awful warnings in the pamphlet (if indeed he ever clapped eyes on such a document), but he was made painfully aware of them by the drill instructor, who must have known them by heart. Normally, they were not patiently pointed out as if by a considerate teacher; they were shouted. We are back to the noise factor again.

Whatever he had to do may have involved some ordinary explanation to begin with, but the practice of the required movements brought about a considerable increase in volume. With foot drill – at ease, attention, left turn, right turn, about turn, quick march, slow march, open order, close order. With rifle drill – order arms, slope arms, present arms, port arms, trail arms, change arms, reverse arms (the funerals again). To say nothing of the ramifications of fixing and unfixing bayonets.

He soon found out that every single movement – whether of foot drill or rifle drill, but obviously more with rifle drill because of the extra component involved – carried endless 'common faults'. These ran a fearsomely wide gamut – from bending backwards, moving the eyes, not keeping arms straight, letting elbows stray from sides, swaying the body, peering to make sure, swinging the arms the correct distance, to 'dropping the right shoulder to the rear' (which sounds difficult enough when you are doing it deliberately, never mind by accident).

This portfolio of evidence should help to show that 'square-bashing' was no doddle. Getting it right was a matter of constant practice, endless effort, aching muscles, bruises and sprains, red faces, bafflement, and exasperation. Like almost everything else, when you see it done well, it doesn't look very difficult. But, if you don't believe there is anything much in it, just try.

However, practice usually made, if not perfect, then a great deal better. Drill sergeants – the good ones – worked as hard as their charges too. They were human (despite what their squads thought of them at times); they wanted to produce the best platoon in the company or the Depot or whatever. They may have shouted and sworn, but their invective and their blasphemy usually had a purpose. Again – with the good ones – it was usually rationed, and often doled out with a dollop of humour as well.

They took pride in doing a good job, just like anybody else.

If they were good at moulding their platoon into a working team, they found that some of this pride could rub off on them too. This was one of the great surprises of basic training. If anyone had told recruits, six or seven weeks before, that they would get satisfaction out of square-bashing, they would have regarded the speaker as a lunatic.

But the fact had to be accepted that there were moments: on a crisp November morning, when the hands were all striking the rifles together, and the boots all hit the ground at the same instant; when you *knew* it was going right. It *felt* right. You knew the sergeant had done his job; for just a few moments, he wasn't such a swine after all.

CHAPTER 14
Polishing Plimsoles

The biggest ignoramus in the world knew that members of the Armed Forces lived active lives. He understood therefore that they had to be in a pretty fair state of fitness in order to be able to perform all those physical feats required of them on active service. He had not sat down and worked this out after several hours of contemplation; it was a vague general impression that he had absorbed from simply being alive and keeping his eyes open – rather as he appreciated that jugglers had to practise a lot or that doctors had to undergo several years of training before they were let loose on the general public.

It followed then that the National Service recruit expected to be given a measure of physical training. He may not have been looking forward to it; there were plenty of young men who, once they had left school and were free from the demands of the school P.E. teacher, made a vow never to go near a gym thereafter. They were non-benders; they were sports-haters; they were cursed with two left feet and no ball sense; or they were just plain lazy. Their only exercise was moving from one chess table to another or swapping the public bar for the more plush surroundings of the saloon bar.

He may not have known much about it either; his only expectation was that the Army, or the Navy or the Air Force, was going to get him fit – whatever that meant. Here is another instance of the difference between British life in 1948 and British life now, over sixty years later.

The public then was not bombarded with dire warnings about unhealthy living. It was not constantly supplied with figures about blood pressure and cholesterol. Few took the trouble to avoid carbohydrates because most people had not the faintest idea what a carbohydrate was. Tables and shelves in bookshops were not groaning under the weight of books about diet and foreign cooking. A lot of people smoked because they had not made the connection between tobacco and cancer (indeed few recognised medical authorities had yet suggested it). Words and phrases like 'fatty secretion', 'white meat diet', 'jogging', 'life style', 'circuit training', 'blood pressure monitors' did not exist.

You could not go out into the high street and buy enough home gym equipment to stock a medieval torture chamber. You did not spend a large slice of your fat senior executive income on a personal fitness adviser (or, if you prefer, 'advisor'). You did not train for the London Marathon every year; it wasn't there. You did not go orienteering; it had not been invented. You did not go in for triathlons; they had not been invented either. The Olympic Games themselves had only just been revived after the War, in 1948. A dozen sports which now figure regularly on the Olympic programme had not been devised. Even those who prided themselves on playing a team game every Saturday only turned up on Saturday afternoon, played till they were puffed, had a shower, a few beers, and several cigarettes, and reckoned that they had spent the day well.

Physical education, then, just after the War, was, if not a closed book, little more than a muzzy recollection of jumping around under the eye of a schoolteacher. The Depot gymnasium and its instructors were going to give many recruits a sharp surprise. Even those who reckoned that they were 'pretty fit' were going to get one as well.

The actual P.E. kit itself, however, was what everyone expected – shorts, vest, socks, plimsoles. The Army provided it, with that individual twist that they put on all their kit.

The shorts were on the baggy side; the socks were the same prickly ones that they wore for other activities; the vests were of two colours – 'Vests PT red' and 'Vests PT white'. Why two colours were necessary was never made clear.

With what might have been construed as consideration for welfare came the issue of a sweater as well, for use outside in cold weather. How kind of the Army. This impression vanished as soon as one put it on. It was constructed of a truly teeth-grinding hairiness which would have made a medieval martyr wince. Even if you wore a 'Vest PT' underneath, there wasn't much of it, and the pressure of the sweater against wide expanses of bare skin had to be experienced to be believed.

Finally, there were the plimsoles. As suggested above, the Army had a way of giving even these harmless items a twist of their own; in many units it was common practice to insist that the owners of these plimsoles should polish them. They were brown on issue; recruits were made to use *black* shoe polish, *on the canvas* of the uppers, and *make them shine*. If ever the dictionary was right on the ball with a definition, it was here with the word 'bull' – to 'meet excessive standards of neatness'.

Once the actual activity began, though, one had to hand it to the Services that they went about their task of turning a platoon of reluctant young men of every size, shape, and suitability into something resembling a fit unit with commendable skill and professionalism.

Few were particularly muscular. Their universal youth by no means meant that they were all naturally athletic. The author trained in a platoon over twenty per cent of whom wore glasses, and not just for reading. Some had not yet reached their full height and maturity. Indeed, there were instances where one could monitor the growing fitness of a recruit almost week to week: his chest developed; his cheeks filled out; his stoop was cured; his stamina doubled; he grew taller, and fatter. The fact had to be admitted: the Forces were good at it.

So were their instructors, upon whom the whole system depended. Again, there must have been variations, but the overwhelming evidence seen by the author was that the level of teaching was very good. There was no fuss; there were no histrionics; you ended up by wanting to do well when they were watching you.

Nor was there the concomitant hectoring, bawling, bullying, and swearing usually associated with NCOs. This is probably explained by the fact that these men were concerned with the physical safety of twenty-odd young men jumping, climbing, vaulting, and generally careering around in an enclosed space with a lot of heavy apparatus everywhere.

They looked the part too. Clothes were always spotless and well fitting. Their limbs were of such a knotty muscularity that when they walked or jumped or demonstrated anything, they seemed, like ballet dancers on a distant stage, to have no weight. They explained untheatrically; they watched patiently; they encouraged in a deadpan sort of way; and they didn't miss a thing.

They fitted so ideally into their surroundings that it became difficult to imagine them doing anything else – rather as one could not easily imagine one's dentist on the golf course. If a recruit had chanced to meet one of his corporal instructors coming out of a tube train on the Bakerloo, he would have expected him to be wearing a skin-hugging white singlet and dark, tapering trousers with elastic bands under the instep.

So the recruit learned how to forward rolls and backward rolls. He did things he never expected on the wall bars. He summoned up his courage to vault over the 'long horse' – with varying degrees of success. He tried to heave himself up to and over huge wooden beams. He struggled to climb ropes. The Army had a favourite test for this (and almost certainly the Navy too; with their venerable tradition of shroud-clambering, they must have had many more elaborate ones). The recruit was required to climb a rope and come back down again *twice* – without touching the floor between the first and the second. It was the second ascent that killed you.

That took care of the internal stuff. The Great Outdoors awaited. There were tests for that too. Basic training protocol required that you high jump a certain number of feet, that you long jump many feet more; that you run a mile in about six minutes. This may sound pretty small beer when we are used nowadays to miles being run in barely more than three and half. But this was the decade – the 1950s – when the four-minute barrier was broken for the first time. Even so a reader might still scoff and think that six minutes is more than enough. Once again, if he feels like that, the author politely suggests that he might like to try.

There was one other rather engaging component of basic physical training – the lift. Or rather the fireman's lift. No doubt this was everyday stuff to your average fireman, but it was new to everybody else apart from the occasional film hero rescuing his beloved friend from the burning building.

It involved carrying somebody else over the shoulder for, say, a hundred yards, in a certain time – about a minute. So, again, you didn't have to be Tarzan.

But what you did have to do was get the body on to your shoulder. You worked in pairs, and took turns to be the lifter and the dead body. The 'dead body' was under instructions to act real dead, with limbs and heads flopping all over the place. Once again, if anybody thinks this is a piece of a cake, let him find a floppy friend and try.

Finally came the Big One. Everyone was required to run a mile in full battle order in eight minutes.

This first requires an explanation of what was meant by 'Battle Order', which takes us back to the day when the recruit was issued with all his kit. Part of that kit – a very large part of it – consisted of a bewildering mass of webbing and buckles and flaps and studs.

The basis of it all was the belt. There was only one size, but the design of it allowed enormous variation, to accommodate everything from the waist of the slenderest Kitchener drummer boy to the overhanging paunch of the fattest quartermaster. On the front of it were to be attached two ammunition pouches, with buckles on the top. On the back of the belt were two more buckles. Straps were fixed to these buckles, taken crosswise over the shoulders and down to fit into the buckles at the top of the pouches.

Then, on to the back was slung one of the packs, which were further anchored by yet more buckles which were attached to the top of the pouches. This was supposed to keep the pack from slipping too far backwards towards the hips. Unfortunately, if the pack contained everything that regulations demanded, the weight caused it to drag the pouches up towards the chin, to form a sort of webbing brassiere. The only way to counteract this was to pull the belt in so tightly that the sufferer found himself wearing something tighter than an Edwardian dowager's corsets. Not exactly ideal.

This was 'Battle Order'. The ensemble was completed by the tin hat on the head. This was also constructed in the belief that every soldier's head was uniformly spherical – presumably a relic of Oliver Cromwell's New Model Army. To be fair, there was some padded leather lining, with a minimum of adjustability. Finally came the nine-pound Lee-Enfield rifle slung over a shoulder. This weapon had a noble lineage too; it was the weapon whose cartridges had helped to spark the trouble which led to the Indian Mutiny. Army kit – you had to admit – was made to last.

This was what the recruit had to put on before he could make an attempt on the 'mile in eight minutes' which the tests demanded.

If he could do that, he could bask in the satisfaction that he was what the Army called 'physically fit'.

CHAPTER 15
Playing for the Regiment

The Army, the Navy, and the Air Force were crackers about sport. Why should these organisations, dedicated to conducting wars, be so keen on playing games? What is the connection between the sporting spirit and killing people?

Soldiers, sailors, and airmen fight. That's what they are there for. When the Government decided to conscript all those young men from civilian life for two years 'with the colours', as some publicists romantically called it, they did not do it in order to put some backbone into the effete youth of the day, to build their characters, to make them self-reliant and useful citizens. The Boys Scouts did that, along with countless other nationwide organisations with the worthiest of motives.

No. The Government did it because they were short of soldiers, sailors, and airmen. As previously explained, there was an empire to run, and several wars to be fought. Perhaps wisely, the journalists did not call the Second World War 'the war to end wars'. Just as well. Perhaps they had learned their lesson. At any rate, in the decade or so after 1945, British servicemen found themselves fighting in Palestine, Cyprus, Malaya (as it then was), Egypt, Kenya, and above all in Korea. There were 'trouble spots' too in places like Trieste, Greece, Indonesia, Vietnam, and Hong Kong – where British troops *might* be needed – to say nothing of the permanent frontier zone patrolled by the North Atlantic Treaty Organisation against the wicked Communists (this swallowed up countless British troops for years). Prime Minister Attlee and his cabinet had to honour their promise to release all the hundreds of thousands of servicemen after their wartime loyalty and sacrifice, and something had to be found to fill their place, given the commitments outlined above. Hence National Service.

It so happened that in the process two and half million young men did have some backbone put into them, did have their characters built, and did become useful citizens afterwards – well, quite a lot of them anyway. But behind it all was the clear truth: they were there to fight a war if necessary.

The Imperial General Staff and the Admiralty and the Air Ministry never lost sight of that fact. Everything a national serviceman did, or was trained to do, was geared to the possibility that he might one day find himself engaged in hostilities. This explains why the vast majority of them were drafted into the Army, because it would be the Army which would do most of the fighting. Moreover, the Navy and Air Force were becoming so increasingly technical that they needed more specialists; there was less room for the uneducated and unemployed and unemployable. One thing the Army could do, and do well, was to take the most unlikely of young men – feed them, clothe them, house them, educate them, train them – and turn them into effective soldiers.

So young men were trained to be fit and to handle the basic weapons, gadgets, vehicles, or whatever of their particular section of the Services. They therefore had the knowledge, and their bodies had been built up sufficiently to be able to deploy that knowledge to the best effect.

That was not enough. That took care only of the bodies and the brains; it did not develop the mind or the spirit. Anybody in charge of any human group knows that, given that knowledge, numbers, physical fitness, and equipment are equal, the unit which succeeds is the one with the highest morale. And one of the best ways of building morale is through sport, particularly team sport. Hence the Services' near-obsession with it. At the risk of sounding trite, a team depended on a group of individuals working together, and wanting to work together. Each individual contributed his particular skill or aptitude, but the effect of their joint contributions amounted to more than simply adding up their individual contributions. As Kipling put it, 'The strength of pack is the wolf, and the strength of the wolf is the pack.'

Field-Marshal William Slim, reckoned by many to be the finest British fighting general to come out of the Second World War, wrote a book called *Defeat into Victory.* It was about his campaign in Burma against the Japanese. When he took over command, the Fourteenth Army was at its lowest ebb. Morale was at rock bottom. The Japanese were regarded as undefeatable jungle supermen.

Slim realised that it would not do to build the army's numbers, fitness, and equipment if they still thought they were not good enough. He had to give a great deal of attention to building morale. He toured endlessly to the most distant and humble groups, making innumerable informal speeches. He devoted a memorable chapter to writing about it. With many of his less sophisticated units, he said he continually used the metaphor of the mechanical watch or clock. No single component drove the clock, but each was vital because, if it should stop, everything was so closely enmeshed that it would interfere with the workings of all the rest, and the whole clock would stop.

His book was much admired by his fellow-professionals, and was taken up by those responsible for Services training. The parallel with a sports team was clear. Sport was seen as very enjoyable. It followed then that something enjoyable like this was to be encouraged. The Forces, for once, could offer something that everybody liked doing, away from the parade ground or the firing range or the workshop or the gym. And without their realising it, it would have such value in the unmentioned, but very serious business of waging war. Well, that was the thinking.

Of course, Slim and his book were not the only generators of this philosophy, but they gave a great boost to it and to its spread. Wherever British Forces units were stationed, at home or abroad, there were games, especially team games – chiefly of course cricket, football, rugby, and hockey.

Army companies had their teams. So did battalions, regiments, brigades, divisions, armies, squadrons, air groups, shore stations, ships, fleets, everybody. One could fill every illustrated page in this book with countless photographs of young men in shorts, with carefully-folded arms so that they emphasised their biceps, in front of aeroplanes, regimental flagpoles, barrack blocks, cricket pavilions, marquees, flight decks, tented camps, and just about any open space where a set of goalposts could be erected, a field marked out, or a set of stumps banged into the ground – anywhere from Norway to the Tropics, from tundra and desert to forest and jungle, in any weather conditions from wind and ice to post-monsoon sunshine.

Officers' messes, sergeants' messes, wardrooms, squadron headquarters, NAAFI canteens, were festooned with plaques, shields, cups, medals, flags, and pennants marking a host of successes over rival regiments and ships and territorial units – anybody within striking distance. Sport was usually considered so important that transport to quite far-away places was made available. Red tape mysteriously unwound itself and disappeared. No cost was too high if it meant inflating the unit's opinion of itself.

Any young man in the Services who displayed sporting prowess soon found that his prowess was going to be encouraged, developed, and exploited. Barriers were removed; time off was facilitated; travel permits materialised. Perhaps even promotion was on the cards. From humble beginnings with his depot team, he could find himself in the brigade team, in the area team, in the command team. That was just the foothills; before long he would be scaling the heights of the Army itself, or the Navy, or the RAF. Finally, he could trot out at Wembley or Twickenham for the Combined Services.

He was part of the whole climate of rivalry which dominated the Forces. Much of it might be hidden from the general public, who understood little beyond the fact that the three Armed Forces were different, and therefore likely to be in competition with each other. Again, it was part of the psychology. Competition engendered effort, urgency, passion, desire to be the best – all vital to fighting efficiency. Slim ended his work leading the Fourteenth Army in Burma with his men actually believing that they had the beating of the Japanese.

So, added to the natural rivalry between the Army, Navy, and Air Force, was a whole jungle of competition at lower levels. Brigades and divisions. Above deck crews and below deck crews. Highland regiments and Lowland regiments. Heavy infantry and light infantry. Sappers and gunners. Corps and regiments. Air crew and ground crew. Infantry and cavalry (that is, tanks). Fleet Air Arm and submariners. And everybody against the Guards.

There were minority sports too – ski-ing, swimming, boxing – any activity where athletic skill could be displayed and team spirit built.

National Servicemen found that their talents too could be harnessed. They found also that, if they were good, little discrimination was shown against them. It was their talent that mattered. Niceties of rank were of course observed at all times, but, so long as the soldier or sailor or airman behaved himself, he could feel confident that no level of competition was barred to him because of his rank or because of his status as a non-regular.

Because there were so many of them, the Services must have benefited enormously because of this vast new reservoir of sporting talent that was suddenly made available to them through an Act of Parliament. This must have been particularly evident when so many young graduates, their period of postponement having expired, brought an extra three years of strength and experience to their teams.

Welcome too was the democratic spirit at large in the various teams which played regularly in thousands of depots and barracks and squadrons and shore stations and distant colonies and border posts and desert encampments and bush headquarters and field detachments. Regulars and recruits fielded alongside each other in the slips; privates and WOs took turns to take penalty kicks; NCOs and officers supported each other in the scrum.

It was true that the captain was usually the highest-ranking member of the team, but – well, it was still the Armed Forces.

Nevertheless, it sometimes gave the lowlier members a chance to get their own back. If a particularly unpopular corporal, or an especially obtuse subaltern, was in the opposing team, a few well-placed elbows or a couple of carefully-timed tackles could help to pay off some long-kept scores. And it was all accepted as 'part of the game'.

'Playing the game' made it all a curious echo of the Edwardian public-school ethos. The Forces, especially the Army, seemed to be stuck in a minor time-warp in their attitudes. The formality – you could tackle a major, send him flying, and maybe haul him to his feet, then say 'sorry, sir'. The democratic philosophy that made you all members of the same team – but privates were not invited to tea afterwards in the officers' mess. A private could score a century, and have the captain clap him on the back and say, not 'Well done, Frank', but 'Well done, Benson'. It could be jarring. Ultimately, it wasn't easy or natural.

But then, it wasn't sport for sport's sake. It was sport for the sake of the Army, the Navy, or the RAF. One day, perhaps, some members of these teams would be in action together, and they had to get used to relying on each other, to the extent of entrusting their lives to each other. It was all a means to an end.

Of course, the average national serviceman did not see it like that. He was not aware of the big picture; even if he had been, he would not have been interested. All he knew was that, if he was good at sport, a whole world of opportunity could open up before him. If you could catch a ball, or kick one, suddenly the next twenty months were not going to be all bull and blanco.

WAITING

When basic training was over, one did not always move on straight away to a permanent posting. A lot of time was spent cooling the heels in the Depot. One remedy was to promote them lance-corporals – temporary, acting, unpaid of course – and put them to work in a variety of humdrum jobs in the attempt to keep them out of mischief. They were warned by the Commanding Officer to take their new promotion seriously, and to make their friends in future among the corporals.

This page and opposite: *The Services took its sport very seriously. Games which had been arranged were to be played regardless of the weather – in this case arctic. Competitions, cups, and medals were continual. The spectators were not there from keenness; it was simply that there was nothing else to do.*

CHAPTER 16
Just Like John Wayne

National Servicemen did not know much of what to expect when they were conscripted, but one thing they could feel fairly sure about was the fact that they would be called upon to fire guns. Indeed, they were so bewitched by the exploits of war film heroes that firing guns was perhaps one of the few things they might have been looking forward to. The sharpshooting pistols, the grenades fastened to the lapels of the combat uniforms, the inexhaustible machine gun magazines – it all looked mighty tough. Certainly worth having a go at.

It was puzzling, therefore, that the Forces seemed to take such a long time before they got around to allowing such an adventurous luxury. Recruits learned how to slope rifles, order rifles, port them, carry them, present them, change them from one shoulder to another (and of course clean them – endlessly). They practised with the five drill rounds with which everyone was issued. They learned how to take a Bren gun to pieces, and put it together again. They were given lectures on the insides of hand-grenades. Anything, it seemed, but actually fire them or throw them.

(This chapter, incidentally, is concerned only with the basic military weapons, mostly used by infantry, though no doubt thousands of sailors and airmen were made familiar with at least the rifle and the light machine gun – of which more later. So there will be no account here of training in weapons which might have been familiar to, and peculiar to, the Navy, the RAF, the Artillery.)

Of course the time came soon enough. A feature of Forces life – for recruits – was the fact that there was so much fresh, and startling, experience packed into such a short period. This produced a double view of their lives. When they looked back, they were often surprised that so many weeks had gone by. But looking ahead was a different matter. There were so many new lessons, new tests, new exercises, new challenges, new frightening prospects looming that a week ahead could seem like a month. The end of basic training could shimmer on the future horizon as distant as the Second Coming.

The prospect of their first outing on the range was viewed therefore with a mixture of relief and apprehension. Relief that they were, at last, about to do something logical, and something that they had always fully expected to do. Apprehension because they had found out a thing or two about the weapon they were going to fire. They already knew it was heavy, and awkward, and that it had nasty projections all over the place.

Rumour and exaggeration now combined to embellish the image of the rifle with all sorts of frightening dimensions which almost turned it into a potential instrument of torture.

Its age, for a start. The ancestor of the Lee-Enfield rifle had first seen the light of day in time to be responsible for some of the tension that led up to the outbreak of the Indian Mutiny in 1857. It was so called because the inventor of its bolt mechanism was a Mr James Lee, and the weapon was built at the Royal Small Arms Factory at Enfield. The .303 version been adopted in 1895, and had seen regular service right through two World Wars. It was to continue in use right through the period of National Service. (According to one authority, the Indian Police are still using it.)

With youth's wariness of anything remotely old, one wonders how much respect they would have had for this venerable relic from the nineteenth century.

Worse, this weapon did not only have the doubtful reliability of age; it had age's cantankerousness. Rumour had it that the recoil of discharge was capable of shattering a jaw or breaking a collar-bone. Its report could burst an ear-drum. Its liveliness could bruise cheeks and cause podgy swelling.

It didn't help, either, when, on the first day they went to the range, they were issued with ammunition which had dates like '1943' and '1944' stamped on it. Could gunpowder last effectively all those years? No recruit had any idea.

The Army were great ones for making do and, if not mending, at any rate sticking with what you knew. Rifles out of the Boer War. Bullets out of the Normandy landings. Webbing which had the weariness and wrinkles of age all over it. (Webbing was indestructible.) The kit which a soldier had to wear for shooting on the range – belt, ammunition pouches, and cross straps – was known universally as 'Musketry Order'. Was this a relic from the Peninsular War? When, later, they were taken to chilly beaches on the Kent coast for long-range shooting, they were issued (for the day only) with leather jerkins which made them all look like a batch of archers lining up at Agincourt. The Forces liked to make things last.

Perhaps in the case of National Service, it was a case, not only of making do, but of organising priorities. The Armed Forces in the 1940s and 1950s had a huge number of commitments, and the country had only just emerged from a crippling war. Everything was tight; everything was in short supply. So – at a guess – the needs of national servicemen came a long way behind the needs of servicemen on active duties all over the world. Hence the 1943 bullets and the weary webbing.

Possibly with the weaponry too. If the Lee-Enfield and the Bren gun and the Sten gun were doing the job, why divert precious resources into research for more, when there were countless calls on the budget for other things? A definitive answer to all these questions would require a very detailed look into the minutes of the Treasury, the War Office, the Admiralty, the Air Ministry, and the Ministry of Defence.

Be all of that as it may, what concerned the recruit was his first foray on to the 25- yard range at the back of the barracks, where he was to fire his rifle for the very first time. He was afraid. He was afraid of the thing jumping out of his hand, deafening him, and shattering his cheek, his jaw, or his collar-bone all at the same time. His head was spinning with the instructions he had been given in previous 'dry' training about holding the stock 'firmly', looking through the backsight and bringing the foresight correctly into focus, making sure his legs behind him were at the correct angle, placing his cheek alongside the butt, keeping still, breathing correctly, and of course the final exhortation: 'You don't pull the trigger; you SQUEEEEEEEZE it!'

He was so taken up with trying to remember everything he had been told that he often had little or no recollection of actually peering through the sights when he pulled – sorry, squeezed – the trigger.

The range, as explained, was only small. The targets were little bits of paper only 25 yards away. Circles of one, two, or three inches radius gave the proof of how well the recruit performed. If all five shots could be spanned by a ring of one-inch diameter, he was declared to have a 'one-inch group', which was reckoned as not half bad. Two-inch groups or three-inch groups received correspondingly more reserved compliments. There was naturally a good deal of variation. It was not unknown for someone to retrieve a target paper with six shot-holes on it.

By the time he went on to the full-length range, he was of course rather more experienced. However, a new gamut of tests awaited him. He had to learn to fire at 200 and 300 yards' range. He had to learn to aim and fire at a quickly-appearing, and disappearing, target – Snap Shooting. He had to practise getting off five or ten shots in a prescribed number of seconds – Rapid Fire. And so on.

Some of course showed real promise. It may have led, later in their service, to specialised training as a sniper. One or two may have graduated to becoming actual instructors at the Small Arms School. They were the real experts.

Others, like majorities everywhere, did their modest best. In some cases, that was not very good. As mentioned above, in the author's platoon, there were about twenty per cent who wore glasses. One of that myopic number swore that, at 300 hundred yards, far from hoping to get any kind of group, he could not see the target at all.

That took care of the rifle. Then came the Bren gun – officially known as the 'Light Machine Gun'. There had been several tested, but in the 1930s the Army plumped for the Bren. It was manufactured originally in the Czech town of Brno. When the Army bought it, production was transferred to the Royal Small Arms Factory at Enfield. Hence – 'Br' from Brno, and 'En' from Enfield – 'Bren'. It served throughout both World Wars, the Korean War, and was still in use in the Falklands War. It remained active till 1991, and is allegedly still being made in India. Once again, the Army believed in sticking to what you knew.

So, if nothing else, it must have been reliable. And, so far as the author can gather, it was. It weighed a lot – about 25 pounds – and it needed two men to carry all the kit – the gun itself, the spare magazines, and (a rare piece of kit for the battlefield) a spare barrel. It could be fired lying down and from the hip. It could fire single shots and machine bursts. It was very adaptable. Despite its longevity, one rarely heard criticisms of it.

Then came the weapon which everybody wanted to have a go at, because it, or something very like it, figured in so many tough Hollywood war films. This was the Sten gun. Another one christened with a mnemonic. It was developed in the Second World War by a Major Reginald Shepherd and a Mr Harold Turpin, and it was built, once again, at Enfield. Take 'S' of Shepherd, the 'T' of Turpin, add 'En' of Enfield, and there you are – Sten. Its great attraction was its cheapness, and its ease of manufacture. Apparently, at the height of its production, it could be made in five man hours.

It may have appealed to the Al Capone in every recruit's breast, but it was notorious for stopping at the most inopportune moments. However, few recruits saw a great deal of it. The rifle and the Bren dominated.

Some platoons received two or three lessons on the Browning pistol or revolver. They did enough practice, not to become proficient, but enough to realise that it was impossible to achieve the marksmanship of your average western film star or Rider Haggard hero.

That left two weapons, the two-inch mortar and the grenade. Every platoon had a mortar section. The 'barrel' was a tube of two inches' diameter (hence the name). It screwed on to a metal base plate. The 'bomb' (it really did look like a bomb) was slid down into the barrel from the top, so that the detonator rested down against the dormant firing pin. You 'pointed' the barrel at an angle of anything from 45 to 90 degrees according to your estimate of the distance required (it could reach 500 yards), you leaned away, and somebody pulled a lanyard which drove the firing pin up against the detonator, and away it went – either smoke or high explosive.

So everybody learned that.

Finally came the hand grenade – yet another 'John Wayne' weapon. But not so enjoyable when you were in the throwing bay pulling out the pin, and holding the rod which prevented the detonator being set off. God – suppose you dropped it! But the sergeant instructors were more than equal to the occasion. No bawling or swearing here. Just sound, solid, almost grandfatherly advice and encouragement. Nerves of steel. The Army knew when to shout and when not to.

CHAPTER 17
Little Circles

Whether a recruit liked it or not (and he usually didn't – at any rate not to begin with), the Army, and the Navy, and the Air Force were working on him. An Act of Parliament had not put him in the Armed Forces simply so that those Armed Forces could push him around, give him thousands of piddling little things to do, force him into lung-bursting physical exertion, deprive him of scores of home comforts, and generally make him fed up.

Had he but known – had he been able to look up just a little from his ditch of deprivation and slough of self-pity – he would have noticed an irony in the situation: not only did he not want to be in the bloody Army; the Army didn't particularly want him either.

Regular soldiers, and sailors, and airmen, were what it said – 'Regulars'. Professional. They had signed on for several years. They meant it. Dammit, they liked it!

Moreover, they had signed on with the expectation that they would quite probably see some action. Proper action in a proper war. Or at least a campaign. Very different from 2012, when the news is full of the activities of terrorists, freedom-fighters, ethnic cleansers, insurgents, pirates, hardliners, militants, extremists, rebels, drugs barons, suicide bombers, local tribal leaders, war lords, and generally pretty unsociable people.

Suddenly, all those regulars found themselves the victims of a random Act of Parliament, which decreed that every fortnight, 6000 unwilling young men would be hoicked off the streets, bundled into uniform, and trained to be fighting servicemen. And it was up to them – the regulars – to train them. This was anything but what they had signed on for.

But they were what it said: 'Regulars.' Professional. They were there to do what His Majesty or Her Majesty ordered them to do, through his or her elected government. Above all, they were there to respect the sacred nature of command. So whether they liked being swamped by these spotty-faced amateurs, with their moaning and their long faces, was beside the point; they had to lump it and get on with it.

To the great credit of most of them, they did. It was the same with their superior officers and the high command. There may not have been many dashing Hannibals or Alexanders among them, but there were lots of seasoned, conscientious men who took a pride in their profession, and who did their best.

Many of them had seen action in the War; there were still plenty of DSOs, DFCs, and MCs on chests. MMs and DCMs too. The author worked with one sergeant-major who wore a medal ribbon from the North-West Frontier of the 1930s.

These men, both officers and NCOs, understood perfectly well why that Act of Parliament had been passed, and they turned manfully to the business of carrying out its terms. In short, they had to turn 6,000 young civilians arriving every fortnight into trained, effective service personnel.

Initially, and obviously, it was necessary for a soldier to be physically able to carry out his duties should Fate place him in an area of hostilities.

So, as has been recorded, every national serviceman had been given a medical examination even before he walked through the barrack gate. It is worth noting, incidentally, that, if any national servicemen fell ill or was injured, the full range of Services medical facilities was at his disposal – free, for nothing (even before the NHS swung into action).

There were plenty of instances where these facilities proved superior to what he had been used to in his civilian life.

It has been explained too that the physical training he received – both indoor and outdoor – 'built him up'. The cross-country runs, the forced marches, the excursions in full battle order – all added to the strengthening process. Even the countless hours of drill on the square taught him muscular co-ordination, discipline, and stamina, and improved his powers of alertness and concentration. The innumerable sporting activities added their ten per cent.

It seems fair comment that by the end of his basic training, the average national serviceman was immeasurably, and unarguably, fitter than he was at the start.

That was far from the end of it. Suppose a soldier, or sailor, or airman, fell ill? After all, they might be called on to serve in any of dozens of remote, inhospitable, and dangerous places. There were lots of very nasty diseases you could catch. Hence the recruit soon made the acquaintance of the preventative side of medicine. In military parlance, 'Jabs'.

You could be, and usually were, inoculated against tetanus, typhoid, polio, yellow fever, and a terrifying roster of hideous complaints, which, so far as the national serviceman was concerned, seldom got nearer to him – thank God – than the pages of a medical dictionary. But the Forces were taking no chances. The recruit was certainly given no choice. Little sympathy was given to needle-phobia or to the chills of waiting in a winter queue, or to the conveyor-belt techniques employed by weary doctors.

As often as not, once he had recovered from the pain of the actual jab, he had to face the after-effects, which could be much more uncomfortable than the needle – the feverishness, delirium, and general just-let-me-die sick feeling that could last through a whole night and into the next day.

Further thought was given – this time to the very serious business of Temptation. Suppose these pink-cheeked teenagers fell into the clutches of Scheming Women? Worse still, of Loose Women? Suppose they Got into Trouble?

The authorities didn't set much store in the preventative effect of cigarettes and cosy chats with the Padre, and tended to prefer the Scare-the-Daylights technique.

Platoons were herded into a blackout-curtained Nissen hut and regaled with specially-prepared films which illustrated, in minute and stomach-churning detail (and perhaps in colour) what could happened to you if you caught venereal disease. How effective was this po-faced propaganda? Did any recruits about to embark on the thrill of a lifetime suddenly decide to change their mind and ask the lady to put her pants back on? It is unlikely that we shall ever know.

That took care of just about everything the Forces could think of in the way of protecting a soldier's life and health. But supposing nothing worked? After all, in action, the enemy had a nasty habit, quite often, of killing you.

The authorities were ready for that too. It was of course perfectly natural that a soldier about to move into a war zone should want to make a will. That was his own business. But there was the business of your actual body. One of the countless things a recruit had to stamp his number on was a metal identity disc, which he had to wear thereafter on a cord round his neck.

With a rare gesture towards personal feelings, the Forces decreed that, in addition to the soldier's name and number, his religious faith should be banged into the metal. This was, presumably, to ensure that, if by chance, a military padre of your religious persuasion happened to be present at your demise, then you could be consigned to your final resting place according to your preferred ritual.

But that was as far as it went. The military passion for rigid classification then came into play: a soldier was given two choices – 'C. of E.', or 'R.C.' Note the full stops. There was to be no messing about with pettifogging denominational loyalties – no Methodists, no Baptists, no Episcopalians, no Mormons, nothing. You were either 'C.of E.' or you were

'R.C.'. The author saw only one digression from this: one of his platoon was allowed to put 'A.' instead. For 'Atheist'. One wonders what ritual was to be prescribed for him in the sad event of his premature passing.

One wonders too, nowadays, whether Hindus or Moslems or Buddhists have to choose between 'C.of E.' or 'R.C.' They certainly wouldn't choose 'A'.

So much, then, for the needs of the body and of the soul. But care had to be provided for the spirit too. This point has been mentioned in Chapter 15.

National servicemen were young. They were totally inexperienced in military matters. They were not volunteers either. So, at various times, they got fed up; they got lonely; they got homesick; they got depressed. They got bolshie too; they got rebellious; they got cussed. They got into bad habits if not constantly watched and disciplined.

Being young and impressionable, and cut off from regular contact with the outside world, they were easy prey to the great ghost Rumour that stalked every barracks and dockyard and airfield. We have already met the awesome injuries that could be inflicted by the firing of the rifle. One could add the horrors awaiting the unready on the open range, in battle camp, 'on detachment', at a selection interview. One universal legend was the Bromide Spectre. This was the dark suspicion that 'they' put bromide into your tea in order to Dampen the Sexual Desires.

Many recruits were in a worse state than merely impressionable. Some had decided that national service was terrible, and set out to prove it. They put up a large piece of paper inside their locker, with 730 little circles drawn on it to represent each of the days of two years in uniform. Religiously, they ticked off or blacked in a circle every single day.

If you were determined to be miserable, there wasn't a great deal the system could do to help. If you were determined to be bolshie, or cussed, or – worse – to take them on – the system had a great deal they could do about that. With kit inspections, extra drill, cookhouse fatigues, punishment parades, rotten jobs, stoppage of leave, leading in the end to arrest by military police, court martial, and imprisonment (with corresponding stoppage of pay and adding on the extra days of your sentence to your two years), the system usually won in the end. And you were not likely to have become any happier.

Young soldiers and sailors and airmen today would have found much of this more irksome than their counterparts did in the 1950s. They would have had to manage without mobiles, texting, emails, ipads – all the paraphernalia which allows instant communication between pretty well any two spots on the face of the planet. What you never have you never miss.

And, as has already been said, the authorities did try to build morale, because they knew how important it was. Great generals from Marlborough and Wellington onwards have been acutely aware that an army did not run on honour and glory; it ran on regular food and sound tents and punctual wagons with the supplies and letters from home.

The Armed Forces of the 1950s did pretty much the same thing, in their own way. Most young men got fuller and fitter on service training and service food. This in turn made them feel better. Sport played its part (see Chapter 15). The much-joked-about NAAFI did its bit too. NAAFI (pronounced 'naffy', not 'narfy') was the depot shop, in effect. Its facilities were nothing like the wonders trumpeted in the 2012 NAAFI website, but, once again, what you never have you never miss. The 1950s' NAAFI was what the 1950s had – all it had – so the 1950s got on with it.

Curiously, one of the greatest builders of morale was the platoon itself. Twenty-four young men got to know each other extremely well. There were no illusions left after twelve weeks, night and day, exposed to each other. There was no survival without tolerance. People grew to depend on each other. Some grew to like each other. Above all, whether they wanted to or not, they learned to do things together, and they began to take pride in what they could achieve together. Unbeknown to them, a potential fighting platoon was being born.

CHAPTER 18
If it Moves, Salute it

In a Catholic church, a member of the faithful bends his knee to the altar. In many schools, a class of pupils will rise when the headmaster walks into the room. Old-fashioned 'gentlemen' still touch, or even raise, their hats when meeting a member of the opposite sex. In the Armed Forces, all personnel below commissioned rank will salute an officer of any rank, age, or seniority, regardless of their own age or seniority.

We are in the territory of Formality, the world of Official Respect. At its widest, it can be anything from a simple standing up to a full, deafening discharge from a row of enormous cannons. Every large organisation in history has been aware of the binding and awestriking effect of the paying of official compliments. In something like the Armed Forces, whose very existence and survival depend on the centrality of rank and the sacredness of command, it is small wonder, then, that no opportunity is lost to pay these compliments; they emphasise the rank of those involved, and help to cement the principle of automatic obedience which mere rank implies.

Note that it is the rank that is the vital factor, not the bearer of that rank. A gritty sergeant-major is not saluting a downy-cheeked subaltern half his age as an individual; he is saluting the royal commission that the subaltern holds; not the spots on his face, but the pip on his shoulder.

Understandably, therefore, this principle is one of the first that is hammered into National Service recruits as soon as they have learned to put on their sagging denims and oddly-profiled berets, their unpolished cap-badges and their clog-like boots. Officers must be saluted.

The official handbook of drill instructions devotes no fewer than ten pages to this business of what the title of the chapter calls 'Compliments'. With commendable thoroughness it first explains why saluting is done in the way it is: 'The right hand is raised palm to the front and open to indicate no weapon or offensive action; the position of the present arms and the salute with the sword have the same meaning.'

This is a good example of the fact that when the Army (or the Navy or the Air Force) teach you something, they teach you from A to Z. They go right back to basics. Then they go right through, breaking down every movement, or, if it is a complicated movement, every part of that movement. And by the time the NCOs have finished giving you the necessary practice, you are well and truly instructed. When the Army have finished teaching you something like this, you generally stay taught. You might get sloppy or lazy, and you might not do it properly, but you don't forget *how* to do it.

Take the simplest one of all – saluting, at the halt, to the front:

'The right arm is kept straight and raised sideways, until it is horizontal, palm of the hand to the front, fingers extended, thumb close to the forefinger.

'Keeping the upper arm still and the hand and wrist straight, bend the elbow until the forefinger tip of the right hand is one inch above the right eye. Points to note are:-

Upper arm horizontal and at right angles to the side; forearm, wrist and fingers all in one straight line.

Palm of the hand vertical.'

That gets you up there. How do you get down? 'To return to the position of attention the hand is cut the shortest way to the side by dropping the elbow towards the front. The fingers are curled up on the way down.'

There follow nearly half a page of 'Common faults'.

As with so many things people think they know about the Forces. If anyone dismisses saluting as easy, let him try to make the extended forefinger of his saluting arm arrive at a position exactly one inch over his right eye, without, as the book says in its awesome list of faults, 'leaning to the left, straining the muscles and leaning backwards,' or having 'forearm, wrist and fingers not in a straight line'.

Practice, of course, makes perfect, and recruits certainly did a lot of that. And they didn't just do it standing still, to the front. They did it to the side; they did it on the march; they did it with rifles; they did it when 'passing an officer'. That was when they had 'head-dress' on. You were not to salute if you were bare-headed.

However, there were more paragraphs, and therefore more practice periods, learning how to pay the regulation compliments when 'in plain clothes', 'when sitting', when 'without head-dress', 'when addressing or delivering a message to an officer', and so on.

The book thought of everything – what to do when riding a horse, how to salute if your right hand was injured, how to do it on the march – the famous 'eyes right' or 'eyes left', what to do if you were 'driving a mechanical vehicle' (even the Army recognised that this last was a mite dangerous and so excused the driver), how to behave at funerals, paying proper respect to the regimental colours, even what to do if by chance you happened to be in a 'body of troops' which had to pass 'the King, the Queen, and other members of the Royal Family'.

So a National Service recruit had to have his wits about him, especially when, later in his training, he was allowed out in the town, even in plain clothes – just in case he was seen by his Commanding Officer coming out of Marks and Spencer or he bumped into the Prince of Wales out in a pram with his nanny in the park.

But the book was fair too. It stressed once again that the business of saluting was not artifical politeness run riot; it was an integral part of Forces discipline. It specifically stated that 'failure by an officer in uniform to insist on being saluted' was 'a breach of discipline'. It was the officer's fault, not the soldier's. Furthermore, it was an offence by the officer not to return a soldier's salute.

The story was often told about officer cadets on the day of their passing-out parade. The minute the parade was over, they were, officially, officers. The Regimental Sergeant-Major, when he was feeling mischievous, would pass them by and fling up a salute of jaw-dropping rigidity. The poor ex-cadet, conditioned by four recent months of fear and awe of this man, would be in total confusion, and try to slip by as quietly as possibly. The RSM would then shout after them, 'Sir, I am saluting you. Please return my salute – sir!'

One random by-product of this mastery of saluting was that anybody who has been through the saluting regimen not only knows how it should be done, but is instantly aware when he sees it done badly. He can be very critical of film actors who have been badly rehearsed or whose director has no idea at all of how a soldier should really behave. It detracts from the enjoyment of the picture when he sees that the veteran hero of the regiment can't even salute properly.

If saluting was a consuming passion with the Forces, mounting guard was another which ran it pretty close. There cannot be many national servicemen who have not, at one time or another, been called on to be a sentry or a guard.

The first building a visitor sees on arriving at any military establishment is the Guardroom. Every main entrance has guard personnel somewhere pretty close – night and day, seven days a week. Because any military unit in question wants to make a good impression, the soldiers on view are very smartly dressed. If they are not, it will reflect very badly on that unit's reputation. It would be like a slovenly housewife leaving half-open dustbin bags on her doorstep.

So tall peaked caps are in evidence, boots with glass-like toecaps, knife-edge creases in the battledress trousers; and very often white belts and bandoliers instead of the usual khaki. These were usually the provost staff, those specifically responsible for depot discipline. But the rest of the guard personnel was made up of ordinary soldiers, and national servicemen had to do their share.

Nobody ever looked forward to it. You had to be available either all day or all night. If at night, you had to be prepared for several sleepless hours. In theory you did two hours on duty, alternated with four hours off. The reality, in a cheerless guardroom with the minimum of facilities, and the constant coming and going of other guards with boots clumping on a wooden floor (nobody was allowed to take off their boots), meant that sleep was, to say the least, somewhat spasmodic.

A further irony was that everybody had a rifle, but nobody had any ammunition. The only armed member was the guard commander, who sat in the guardroom with a loaded Sten gun, in charge of the pick-axe handles chained to the wall.

Those who had to patrol the barracks inside the curtain wall were each issued with one of these pick-axe handles (or 'Helves pick'). With this questionable armament, the personnel on patrol had to see to the security of arms stores and magazines. Once again, this seems a long way from the constant vigilance that was required when the IRA was in full spate from the 1970s onwards. But in the 1950s, the IRA was barely more than an occasional topic of amused conversation, part of the eternal Irish joke. The danger they were said to represent went little beyond a comedian's footlights quip.

So the average national serviceman's contribution to the security of the realm consisted largely of tugging at the occasional padlock to see that it was still working, and popping into the cellar below the Officers' Mess to top up the boiler.

The great enemy, apart from fatigue, was of course boredom. It was even worse on a weekend guard, when you could be on duty from midday on Saturday to first thing Monday morning. The War had been over for perhaps a decade, maybe more. Whatever other wars were being fought, they were thousands of miles away. The newspapers were not full of headlines about bombs and urban terrorists and insurgents and other disturbers of the peace. The worst you usually got was a column of pacifist anti-nuclear marchers, with college scarves and prams (with babies in), descending upon Aldermaston. It was difficult for a couple of security guards on a summer's evening to feel a sense of urgency when they could hear trolleybuses hiccuping past the barracks front gate. Everything was so normal.

National servicemen, perhaps, did not have the inbred respect that the regulars had, because they were not volunteers. So they thought up ways of passing the time. A favourite one known to the author was home-made golf. The Helve pick was the club. A convenient pebble was the ball. And you did the round of the entire barracks, devising impromptu penalties if the pebble got lost or went down a drain. No doubt several pages could be covered if one were to collect similar reminscences from other patrollers, who, in the author's barracks at least, were known by the unnecesssarily sinister title of 'Prowler Guard'.

Another, perhaps more imaginative, certainly more enjoyable technique was to do what Depot Standing Orders said: examine everybody's identity card – whether they were recognised or not. They could pore over the photograph to ensure that it was a good likeness, or ask the bearer to recite his Army number. And they could hide behind Standing Orders while they were doing it.

The military life can be a combination of hours of intense boredom interspersed by seconds of danger and terror. National servicemen had the good luck, mostly, not to have to suffer the latter.

CHAPTER 19
The Man you Love to Hate

Mention has been made of three favourite clichés of National Service life; the square-bashing, the RSM (or Master at Arms in the Navy and Station Warrant Officer in the RAF), and the bulling. These are the things that everybody who has *not* done National Service thinks he knows all about.

There is a fourth, and everybody thinks he knows about that too. This is the 'Sergeant' – the man who makes you *do* all that square-bashing. In actual fact, it might also be a corporal, or even a sergeant-major at times, but for the sake of simplicity (and space) one has to narrow it down, and personalise it, to one individual. Every national serviceman has had experience of the drill sergeant. No matter what variants of this figure the recruit has suffered under, he will recognise the description and analysis which follows. He will relate to the atmosphere, the philosophy, the approach, the attitude. He will recall the hard work, the fatigue, the frustration, the resentment, even perhaps, at times, the fear. Certainly the wariness and respect that such figures inspire. However well these figures are disguised by the accidentals of a particular time or place, any recruit will Know the Beast.

He is big, loud, unkind, heartless, quite devoid of any Christian virtue, and of doubtful parentage. He makes you do unnatural and irrelevant things, not one of which any soldier or sailor or airman would be called upon to do in a normal war, or even in an abnormal war. His whole existence seems therefore to be devoted to nothing more than making a recruit's life difficult, on the questionable assumption that all this posturing by him and exertion by them, in some incomprehensible way, 'toughens them up'. This whole package is testimony to the total lack of imagination on the part of the Imperial General Staff in that they have been unable, in over two hundred years, to come up with any better way of filling a recruit's mornings.

Why do recruits think like this? A variety of reasons. Ignorance for one. Lack of physical preparedness for another. Lack of mental preparedness for a third – sheer shock. To that one could add fatigue, bafflement, exasperation, and so on right down to petulant self-pity and wilful misery.

Why should this be?

For a start, there is, as explained, ignorance. Recruits had little idea what to expect. Their heads were full of the clichés mentioned above. These clichés jostled in their heads with parental moralising, lurid reminiscence from those who had been in (and come out), heavy-handed humour from so-called friends, and general fear of the unknown. So whatever the Forces were to make them do was going to come as a shock. It is true that the vast majority of national servicemen came, in the end, to take nearly everything in their stride, but they did not do it *at first*.

That is why the recruit's life was so hard; everything was so unexpected. They were the new boys on the block; they were easy meat; they were young; they were easily swayed; they were easily impressed. They were easily *de*pressed too.

When they got depressed, they moaned. Old soldiers grumbled; recruits moaned. Having a drill sergeant around gave them something to moan about; it gave them a focus, a sort of scapegoat. He was the one they saw every day; he was the one who was always making them work and sweat. He was the one doing the shouting and screaming – at *them*.

None of them wanted to be in the Army, or the Navy, or the Air Force, in the first place. They had to lump it, do as they were told. They had to spend hours bulling and running and jumping and pulling triggers and God knows what else. They could not tell a weapon-training instructor what they thought of him; they could not walk into the Orderly Room and tell the Chief Clerk how furious they were at being given a weekend guard duty when they were looking forward to going home for the weekend. They had to take it out on somebody.

So they moaned about the drill sergeant. He was the one who treated them so unkindly, like a gaggle of conditioned zombies – all doing artificial movements in time; slapping rifles; swinging arms to a ridiculous height; the perpetual stamping. Apart from anything else, it was an affront to the dignity. The drill sergeant became the ogre who dehumanised you.

Some of their moaning might well have been justified. Because human nature is infinitely variable, there were bound to be bad drill instructors, incompetent drill instructors, ineffective drill instructors. Scattered among these men there were, inevitably, some boors and some bullies. So the stories, retailed in shocked whispers, about moustaches thrust under the nose, about intensely personal insults, about homing in on an individual's unfortunate weaknesses, no doubt contained some truth. Newspapers even today run stories about barrack bullying, some of which has led to death.

But it is not the norm. And the chances are – and here the author sticks his neck out – that the boors and the bullies in the 1950s were not in the majority either. Quite often it is the ones who have most recently come into authority who are the worst at exercising it. It may well be that some of the worst cases involved National Service corporals who misguidedly thought that to be a good drill sergeant one had to be a nasty one.

Sergeants and sergeant-majors had, obviously, been in the Forces much longer. This was particularly the case in the 1950s. When the War had ended in 1945, there were millions of men still under arms. The majority of them, naturally, looked forward to returning to 'civvy street'. There were many, also, who did not. They had joined up as young men, perhaps even teenagers, and often with little previous purpose in life. They had found in the Services the purpose they had lacked; they had found companionship; they had found confidence. By the end of the War, a lot of them had found promotion as well, with the pay and position that that entailed. And after six years of action, a return to what they had so eagerly left behind in 1939 did not seem attractive.

So they stayed on. Many were still there five, ten, fifteen years *after* the War. Some of them saw further active service in the small wars that punctuated the world peace – in Korea, Malaya, Suez, Cyprus, Kenya. There was also the small business of NATO and the Cold War. But most of them found that, part of the time at any rate, they had been saddled with training over two million national servicemen.

These were experienced, worldly professionals. One had only to look at the medal ribbons on the chest. Some had suffered years of misery in German or Japanese prison camps. They had seen the worst bullies in the world. They did not need to take it out on anybody.

They may not have been overjoyed to be stuck with unwilling recruits, but they were, as explained, professionals; they carried out orders; they got on with it. They had been in the Forces long enough to know that the traffic of discipline did not go all one way.

The training book devoted, for example, nearly forty pages to foot drill, but it also devoted over twenty pages to the responsibilities of the drill instructor and to specimen drill programmes. There was a special section entitled 'How to get the maximum out of a squad'. There was provision made to ensure that NCOs were kept up to the mark with their own appearance and bearing, with their command of the drill movements, and with the actual issuing of orders.

Rules in a book were one thing, and what happened on the square was another. But the important fact was that this was the ideal; this was what the Army *expected*. And no doubt the Navy and RAF too. Rules were not always kept in the Forces any more than they were always kept anywhere else. But having the rules in the book was better than not having them at all.

These veteran NCOs, then, approached the training of a recruit platoon as they approached any other task. Their self-respect, if nothing else, dictated that they should make as good a job of it as they could. If there was more than one platoon in a barracks – and there often was – this meant that one drill sergeant had two or more rivals in the Sergeants' Mess engaged on exactly the same thing. So of course they drove their squads as far as their judgment allowed; they wanted to have the best platoon.

The book got it dead right once again. To get the maximum out of a squad, it said, 'Human nature being what it is, two things are necessary: first the good will and skill of the instructor, and second, since drill is not meant to be easy, ability on the part of the instructor to press the squad up to its maximum capacity.'

Note the perhaps surprising observation that 'drill is not meant to be easy'. And the responsibility placed explicitly on the instructor's shoulders to get the best out of his squad. And, even more shrewdly, lower down the page, it says, 'There is no excuse for pressing a squad beyond their ability to learn or without continuing instruction; this is bullying.'

So if discipline went both ways, and both sides had a part to play, it followed that producing a good drill squad was a partnership. Recruits did not of course see it that way. Not at first. Not perhaps for quite a long time.

What changed their minds? Time – the weeks slowly moulded them. They were bound to. No callow recruit could stand up to all that novelty and exertion for so many weeks and remained unchanged. Secondly, usage. They learned. In time, drill movements became second nature, as they were intended to become. They couldn't do it wrong if they tried. They could do it sloppily, but they couldn't usually do it wrong.

Squad and instructor got used to each other. They had to learn to work together. If, as the book said, good will was there in the instructor, sooner or later he would hope to put it there in his squad as well. If he had half a memory, he would know their names and their individual strengths and weaknesses. If he had half an imagination, he would know when to crack a joke to relieve the monotony. He would build a store of well-honed sallies which kept the wheels oiled. If a recruit in the squad had half a sense of humour, he could liven proceedings with a witty retort or two. Both sides by this time should have built enough confidence in each other to know how far they could go. Even the abuse, if well timed and well applied, with the appropriate garnish of impossible hyperbole, was accepted for what it was – incentive, not mindless obscenity.

Did this mean that recruits got to like drill? Got to look forward to it? Hardly. Did it mean that a drill sergeant leapt at the chance to take over yet another squad of new arrivals for yet another twelve-week stint? Most unlikely. Did every training squad pass all its tests with flying colours, and did they all give their sergeant a cigarette-lighter when they left? No.

But, very often, a drill sergeant took some satisfaction in turning a group of possible likely lads into something resembling a military outfit. And a group of those likely lads found, now and again, to their surprise, that they were taking pride in being better than the other platoons, and that they wanted to put on a good show when they came to do their passing-out parade.

CHAPTER 20
Why Do You Want to Be an Officer?

In the bad old days, boys of twelve could obtain a commission in the Army and the Navy. If there had been an Air Force in the Napoleonic Wars, they would have obtained one there as well. Why? Because their respective fathers had bought it for them. The practice had been in force for a very long time, and received the endorsement of soldiers as gifted and successful (and respected) as the Duke of Wellington. (The Duke had his reasons, and they were not frivolous or selfish, but this book is not the place to discuss them.)

Though the faults of such a practice are obvious, in spite of the weight of the Duke's influence, it survived right up to 1870, when the Secretary of State for War, Edward Cardwell, finally abolished it. Promotion to commissioned rank was henceforth to be on the basis of merit rather than of money or influence.

So far, so good. But that raised the question of how that merit was to be detected, and how it was to be assessed. Especially in embryonic form; judging potential was a very inexact business. If the candidates had signed on for the professional Army (or Navy or Air Force), at least the examiners had the advantage of knowing that they were all keen and committed. With national servicemen this was far from the case; if they had been keen and committed, they wouldn't *be* national servicemen; they would have signed on to be regulars.

So the examiners had the problem of trying to find out what sort of officers these young men would make – young men who, almost by definition, were counting the days to their release from uniform. Training an officer, in any of the three Forces, was an expensive business, involving the commitment of special establishments, buildings, facilities, funds, equipment, and training personnel.

Nor was it a question of promoting national servicemen simply to boss other national servicemen about. (The blind leading the blind, as you might say.) These new officers would be required to serve in regular units, to lead professionals, including NCOs more than twice their age. Possibly in action too.

There was powerful pressure on the authorities to get it right.

The author's experience was in the Army. This represents the experience of over seventy per cent of all national servicemen. As only about two per cent joined the Navy, the number of NS officers there must have been very small, and in any case drafting into the Navy stopped some years before National Service itself did. The author must admit to a gap concerning the RAF, where pilot training must have been highly technical and specialised. There were of course other reasons for officer training there besides flying an aeroplane, some of these technical too. However, there were many common factors in officer-cadet selection and training in all three services. This chapter concentrates on the former. The following three chapters describe the latter. The chances are that any ex-officer-cadet, no matter what colour his uniform, will recognise, and identify with, a lot of what follows.

The first thing for a reader to understand is that the average national serviceman had no idea of the attitude behind what the Armed Forces were making him do. Naturally, he grasped the basic general idea that he was being trained to be a human fighting unit, but it did not go much beyond that.

A classic example of this limited view was the whole business of becoming an officer. He did not know, and he did not much care, what thinking was going on in the minds of the top brass at the War Office. He was not aware of the pressure on them to 'get it right', as explained above.

He may have had a vague idea before he joined up that it might be worth having a bash at becoming an officer. He was worldly enough to realise that nobody *offered* commissions. He was deeply suspicious of all the stories about so-and-so who had 'been offered a commission but turned it down'. The Army may have stopped selling them, but they certainly didn't give them away. There would have to be some tests, some competition, some hard work, but he had little idea of what form it might take.

Fortunately, the Army came to his rescue barely a week after he had arrived. He was told to report to someone called the PSO – yet another service mnemonic which soon assumed a permanent significance. He found out, just in time, that it stood for 'Personnel Selection Officer'. Nowadays, one does not have 'personnel officers'; one has 'Human Resources Directors'. It comes down to the same thing, save perhaps for the fact that the Army PSO was dedicated not to encouraging 'career development', but to weeding out those who were, in his opinion, unfit for it.

In the case of the author, he found that, out of the entire platoon, only one was thus eliminated. All the rest were to be packed off to another unit, where they were to undergo the rest of their basic training (nearly all of it). Moreover, to their surprise, they were to be designated as 'Potential Leaders'. Nobody was sure by what criteria the PSO had done it.

Indeed, for the rest of their basic training, the members of the 'Potential Leader' platoon wondered how and why they had come to be where they were. They liked the use of the word 'Leader'. It sounded more adventurous than 'Officer'. 'Potential Leader' had overtones of Biggles and the Red Baron; 'Potential Officer' sounded too authoritarian for their taste.

But how had their lords and masters arrived at this portentous decision? All they (the 'Potential Leaders') had to rely on was rumour and gossip. Was it because of service in their school cadet force? No, that was clearly not true; many of them had not touched the cadet force with a bargepole. Was it because they had been to public school? Possibly. But there were exceptions to that too. Was it the number of 'O' Levels they had amassed? Was it based on the intelligence tests they had had to sit? Full of odd diagrams and dots and squares, which had not seemed to impose very much on the grey cells. Hardly worth a comparison to Noddy, never mind 'O' Levels. So they were no further forward.

The next hurdle they came across materialised about half-way through their basic training. It was another interview and another mnemonic – USB. It almost sounded like 'Unexploded bomb'. In fact it stood for 'Unit Selection Board'. The Army gave it a fresh twist, in the interests of euphony. A 'y' was stuck on the end, and it emerged as 'USBY'.

It was designed, presumably, to determine whether all that leader potential had evaporated in five weeks, or whether it had in fact enlarged. So the authorities were still taking their responsibilities seriously. In order to emphasise this, the interviews were conducted by a major (the PSO had been a mere captain).

The platoon cottoned on to the idea that this was part of their officer-selection obstacle course, and steeled themselves for a pretty rigorous, and surgically searching, set of tests and questions. The men were going to be sorted out from the boys.

They compared notes afterwards. They were each asked where they had gone to school, how many games they played, and whether they had been a prefect. Tossed in at the end was an enquiry designed to assess their command of current affairs – like who was Jomo Kenyatta, or who the new dictator of Egypt was.

The final weasel question was, very often, why do you want to become an officer? Difficult, this. It was blindingly obvious why most of them wanted to become officers – more money, higher rank, greater privacy and physical comfort, loftier status. But they had enough sense not to say that. One way and another, they cobbled together some vapid verbal confection about service, and making the best of oneself, and the British Empire, or whatever. It was all carefully written down by the Brigade Major, who was probably not fooled by any of it.

If it was meant to be a searching test, it did not seem to have been very effective; in the author's platoon, not a single member was weeded out.

Well, that was Hurdle Number Two. Number Three came fairly soon after the end of basic training. 'Potential Leaders' were required to report to a remote military establishment 'somewhere' in the South of England – for three days of tests.

This concentrated the mind wonderfully. 'Usby' had occupied each of them for about half an hour. The PSO had done his bit in little more than ten minutes. So this one – the War Office Selection Board – inevitably 'WOSBY' – promised to be something along the lines of the Spanish Inquisition at the very least. As the day approached, it was a very rare potential leader who did not go through his share of sleep-stopping worry.

The tests, when they came, were divided roughly into two – outdoor and indoor.

Candidates operated in groups of about five or six. Some were people they knew from their own barracks; some were complete strangers from regiments and units all over the country. They all wore denims. Over their denim top they were required to wear cotton bibs with numbers on them, rather like the old-fashioned footballers or speedway riders. If it was designed to produce anonymity and therefore fairness, it was puzzling that the examining officers, when they addressed their rare remarks to the candidates, did it by means of their names. Yet another baffling feature of Army life.

The tests, when they came, consisted of problems involving planks and tubes and ropes and fences and barrels. Each had a turn as the 'commander', and it was up to him to devise a solution and allocate duties to the rest. While this was going on, three faceless majors and a grim lieutenant-colonel stood about with clipboards and wrote things down on them. They said very little. After each rare success or hapless failure, they exchanged enigmatic glances.

Indoors it was more comfortable, naturally. They wore battledress, and sat in chairs. There were yet more intelligence tests, with the, by now, usual dots and squares and circles.

Then they sat at tables in their fives and sixes, where they were invited to discuss any of a series of current affairs – the Suez crisis, Archbishop Makarios, what were the Communists doing in Malaya, and so on. The problem was not so much thinking of what to say, as working out how to say it, and how much to say. Did you try and impress by holding forth on everything? Or did you cut a dignified figure by sitting quietly and nodding sagely at a well-put point? Whatever you did, or did not do, out came the clipboards, and across the room flew the enigmatic glances.

The next stage put you on a sort of stage – alone. Everybody had to give a ten-minute lecture, on any subject of his choosing. More clipboards.

Finally, the majors and the colonel each put the candidate through yet more interviews. Everybody was asked, four times, whether he had played for the first eleven, if he had been a prefect, why he wanted to become an officer, and who were the candidates in the current American presidential election.

And that was that.

He did not know his fate till he was about to climb on board the lorry to take him to the station the next morning. A piece of paper was given to him (admittedly in a sealed envelope) on which were printed three fates: 'Not recommended'; 'Deferred' (you could have another go in three months' time); and 'Recommended'.

Well, that was how it all seemed to him. The Army may have seen more, but that was their business.

CHAPTER 21

No Such Thing as Bad Soldiers

If you wanted to be a regular soldier – professional, for real – and you wanted moreover to be an officer, you underwent, naturally, a rigorous selection process, involving entrance exams and numerous other tests and interviews. If you were accepted, you attended the Royal Military Academy at Sandhurst (near Camberley in Surrey) for two years.

If you aspired to become an officer during your National Service, you attended WOSBY for three days (see Chapter 20). If successful, your course of training lasted four months.

Officer cadets from the infantry were sent to Eaton Hall in Cheshire; those from the artillery or the armoured corps (tanks, that is) went to Mons Barracks in Aldershot. The author's experience was with the infantry, so the bulk of this chapter will be about Eaton Hall; but, apart from the obvious technical differences in the weapon training, a great deal of what follows will be relevant to the training of all officer cadets.

However, before concentrating on the infantry, it is appropriate to devote just a few sentences to one personality who deserves a mention because he was almost a household name in the 1950s. For several years he was the man in charge of discipline at Mons, so he was a Regimental Sergeant-Major, naturally. He was the senior warrant officer in the whole Army, and his name was Brittain. It was a suitably patriotic name for the jingoistic figure that the newspapers made of him. For RSM Brittain was 'discovered' by the nation's press, who turned him into a celebrity. Photographs of him regularly appeared in the tabloids, in typical bawling mode (bristling moustache, pace-stick, Sam Browne belt and all), with, as often as not, a caption about 'the loudest voice in the British Army'. He even figured in feature films, most famously in one about two Guards officer cadets who subsequently fought, and died, in the last year of the War.

Infantry cadets, then, fresh from their success at WOSBY, turned up at Eaton Hall, near Chester. It was not much like the bleak barracks to which most of them had become accustomed. It was a stately home, no less, and belonged to the Duke of Westminster. It was a vast pile, and stood in an estate of over 11,000 acres.

In fact, only one-eighth of them stayed in the Hall itself, and then only for the last two weeks of their training. The course lasted, as explained, for sixteen weeks, and was divided into eight sections, because a new intake arrived every fortnight. They worked their way up from humble huts to residence in the great man's home in their final fourteen-day session.

These huts were typical enough of the Army, and had been built all over the estate – it seemed. In fact much of the garden area must have been preserved, because the author has a photo of cadets relaxing on flower-bedecked banks besides Wordsworthian lakes. So some care must have been taken by the Ministry of Defence, otherwise His Grace the Duke would not have allowed his property to be taken over for such a long time. Before the Army came in, it had been used for the training of naval cadets during the latter part of the War.

The Duke must have been a very trusting man, because there were several *objets d'art* still about the Hall – statues, gleaming cherubs, even a Rubens or two.

However, barrack life was barrack life pretty much the world over, and newly-arrived cadets soon discovered common factors between what they had been through and what their new acquaintances had been through as well. The Army has a trick of making veterans out of surprisingly short spells of service, because they are so intense.

Cadets soon learned to recognise dozens of cap badges they had never seen before. At one time or another every regiment of the Army must have sent cadets there – the county regiments (for instance the Devons, Dorsets, Cheshires, Berkshires); the 'double' regiments from certain counties (the East Surreys and the Queen's from Surrey, the Royal West Kents and the Buffs from Kent); the light infantry regiments (the Ox. and Bucks., the Durham LI, the King's Own Yorkshire Light Infantry – the 'KOYLIS'); the rifle regiments (the KRRC, the Rifle Brigade); the exotic names (the Green Howards, the Sherwood Foresters); the Celtic fringe (the South Wales Borderers, the Royal Ulster Rifles, the Cameronians); and of course the Guards (always a law unto themselves).

Plumes and bobbles and tabs and bonnets abounded. Cadets had been in the Army long enough to have learned to respect their own cap badge, and this was enhanced in the presence of so many other signs of regimental individuality. It made everybody hold his head up just that little bit higher. Add to that the white tabs which every cadet had to wear on the collar of his battledress (and which had to be 'bulled' to perfection for every parade). It made for a rich mixture indeed. To anyone who remembers the Army like that, it must be a sadness to have witnessed the passing of so much history and tradition and pride – in the name of modernity and economy and 'rationalisation'.

However, no romanticism was allowed to intrude once the training began. It came as no surprise to find that the parade-ground was to figure just as largely as before in basic training. If anything, larger. Maybe not in time, but certainly in intensity. All the drill instructors were from the Brigade of Guards, and cadets soon came to understand why the Guards thought so much of themselves. They really were very good. Their turn-out, their deportment, their words of command were impeccable. When they demonstrated a movement and drove their foot into the ground, you almost winced with the impact.

And that was only the sergeants. When the company sergeant-majors did it, you winced even more. There were four companies on site, with, therefore, four company sergeant-majors. That meant that there was, as usual, only one regimental sergeant-major – thank God. Another guardsman – well over six feet. With his tall peaked cap, he looked over seven feet tall. A moustache – of course. A thick, red neck. Uniform creased like a handful of butcher's knives. Boots like mirrors. And a voice straight from Dante's Inferno. (Brittain wasn't the only bawler by a long chalk.) There must have been quite a few cadets who, if they were honest, would have confessed that the RSM could, and did, inspire physical fear.

There was one feature of the relationship, however, that mitigated against this whole regime of chase and nerves. It was to do with forms of address. Never at any time was a cadet allowed to forget that he was being trained as an *officer*. The problem was, of course, that he was being trained, largely, by non-commissioned officers, men who, as soon as the cadets became commissioned, would become their subordinates. These NCOs had to be allowed to drill their charges, chase them, criticise them, make them get a move on. How did the Army do it?

They did it in two ways. The cadet was instructed to address every NCO instructor, no matter his rank, as 'Staff'. (The one exception, predictably, was the RSM, who rated a 'Sir'.) Every NCO (*including the RSM*) was required to address every cadet as 'Sir'.

This gave rise to the ancient, and no doubt apocryphal, story of the RSM, who used to tell his new arrivals, 'Gentlemen, I call you "Sir" and you call me "Sir". The only difference is, you mean it.'

Well, that may be so, but the arrangement seemed to produce a workable system, which everybody understood.

However, it could give rise to odd dialogue, like:

'You are idle this morning, sir. What are you?'

'I am idle, staff.'

Or:

'Will you get a hold of yourself, sir. Quick sharp, sir. Get a bloody move on, sir.'

All this may seem to some observers like a posturing charade, but there was thought and planning behind it. A working relationship had to be set up, and easily maintained.

Training had to be intensive; these national servicemen had to pack into four months what a regular cadet at Sandhurst was given two years to accomplish. They had to be given enough knowledge to see them through their future service, so that they did not disgrace themselves before their men by their ignorance. They had to be trained in enough skills so that their demonstration of them did not cause hilarity. And they had to be imbued, somehow, with enough genuine military pride to enable them to display some acceptable levels of leadership.

It was no surprise, then, that the Army produced instructors of top quality. Cadets soon realised that, no matter how much they were being chased, they were being chased by the best in the business. Maybe not for a long enough period; there was no way the best instructors in the world could pack two years' work into four months. But what training these young men did receive was good training.

Moreover, it was drummed into them that, as said before, they were going to be officers. They were going to lead men – maybe in battle. More was therefore to be expected from them. It was not enough that they should be able to do everything that their men would be called upon to do; they had to be able to do it better.

To take one example. Their turn-out had to be beyond reproach. It was not enough that their battledress should have all the regulation creases in the right places; they should be noticeably sharper. It was not enough that boots should sparkle; they should dazzle. They were issued with special shirts that had extra buttons that were almost un-do-uppable, so that the collars rested in place with scientific precision – no unsightly curling up at the edges. They had extra tabs on their battledress collars, which were not only white and needed specially blancoing; they had brass buttons on them too.

Ordinary webbing, of course, had to be blancoed to superhuman standards. Any offence or dereliction could lead to show parade, when the offending cadet had to present himself in the early evening carrying the piece of equipment in question, now bulled to celestial brilliance. Further offences, and other crimes of negligence, could be punished with what was called, euphemistically, 'Restrictions.' The culprit had to parade three times a day, outside duty hours, in full battle order, for a complete inspection – of their entire kit. At its worst, it could involve a veritable treadmill of bulling and sweating.

Even that was not enough. Mere blancoing of normal kit would not do. They were also issued with special white equipment – belts and rifle slings. Every Wednesday morning, there was an Adjutant's parade, when these belts and slings (and the white collar tabs) had to be worn or carried. With *white* blanco. Not only on the flat surfaces, but on the edges as well. And God help you if you got some of it on nearby parts of your battledress.

The Adjutant's parade was the high-spot in the disciplinary week. The Adjutant was the officer in any unit responsible for the discipline of that unit; he was so powerful that even the RSM reported directly to him. So, every Wednesday morning, everything – absolutely everything – had to be just right. To make sure of that, every officer or NCO involved in drill or discipline was on parade – Adjutant, RSM, the CSMs, the drill sergeants, everybody. There could be dozens of eyes on you, watching with gimlet sharpness, for any default in dress or drill. This was what was expected of officer cadets.

The same thing applied to their physical fitness, their weapon training, general military knowledge – everything. Good soldiering was born of good officering.

To put it another way, as they regularly did: 'There is no such thing as bad soldiers; only bad officers.'

OFFICER TRAINING

Infantry officer cadets were trained at a stately home near Chester called Eaton Hall, on semi-permanent loan to the War Office from a very rich duke. The great iron frontage was known popularly as 'The Golden Gates'. The vast estate boasted gardens and lakes reminiscent of a Wordsworth idyll.

A pleasant surprise was that the cadets had the run of much of these gardens, and an hour or two spent in them was a treasured oasis of peace in a frantic timetable. Note the formal ties and jackets even in off-duty hours. Cadets in town wearing a coat were required to wear formal headgear.

What everybody knows about, and what they don't. One is the bulling – though it was unusual to be doing it in parade battledress; denims were the normal garb. The thing they don't know is that one picks up all sorts of knowledge from one's barrack mates. In this case, there was a bridge enthusiast, and he got half the platoon at it by the time he had finished.

If the RSM was an awe-inspiring figure in a regimental depot, he was a presence of Baal-like menace and power in an officer-cadet school. This man was well over six feet tall, and built like a steel girder. With the front of his Guards peaked cap rising almost vertical, he looked about seven feet tall. He was capable of engendering true physical fear.

No Army training unit was complete without its assault course, and this was part of it – the fearsome ten-foot wall. Note the obligatory trilby hat for the cadet spectator in civilian dress.

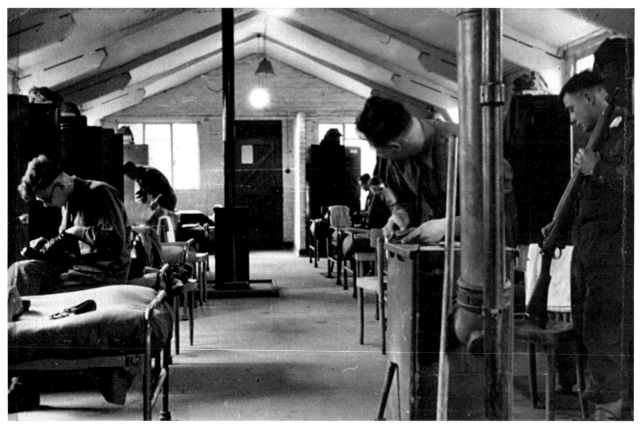

By now the reader should be getting familiar with what a barrack-room should look like. They were much the same wherever you went.

However, there were exceptions, albeit temporary. This was the barrack-room immediately prior to departure to Battle Camp, when the inmates knew they would not be coming back – not to this room anyway. Services life was full of arrivals and departures.

Battle Camp consisted of a fortnight up in the Welsh mountains, and it was extremely vigorous. Incredibly, on a Sunday off, there was enough energy left to wangle a 3-ton truck to take a group even higher up; from there they walked, swam (in a freezing tarn), and climbed to summits – a testimony to the level of fitness the Army had managed to instil.

There was no film company on hand to produce dramatic close-ups of faces, tight belts, and shining boots. But these pictures are more genuine in a way, because this is about as much as the average proud parent saw – and they turned up in droves. Notice that all the women are wearing hats. With the white webbing, the drill, the band, the burning desire to 'get it all right', and the fact that in half an hour's time they would all be officers, it was quite a day.

The finished article – taken for Mum and Dad. Note the shiny new peaked cap. The battledress was a better fit than for other ranks; officer-cadet schools maintained a tailor who produced a much better standard than usual. The Army wanted their junior officers at least to look the part.

The platoon spent the last fortnight of their sixteen weeks in the Hall itself, complete with grand staircase, Rubens, and naked cherubs. Note the inescapable pet dogs with the regular officers. The two guardsmen produced standards of drill and turn-out that no cadet at the outset would have dreamed were possible. They really were the best in the business.

An RAF officer-cadet passing-out parade. The band, the salute, the white webbing, the straight lines – no real difference from the Army.

Despite almost universal aspirations on the part of young RAF officers to become pilots, in fact few of them did so. Weeding-out and drop-out rates were high. But there were alternatives available, as for this group – to be trained in interpreting aerial photographs.

National Service

Elizabeth R

Elizabeth II, *by the Grace of God* OF THE UNITED KINGDOM OF GREAT BRITAIN AND NORTHERN IRELAND AND OF HER OTHER REALMS AND TERRITORIES QUEEN, HEAD OF THE COMMONWEALTH, DEFENDER OF THE FAITH.

To Our Trusty and well beloved   Mark Davis   Greeting:

WE, *reposing especial Trust and Confidence in your Loyalty, Courage, and good Conduct, do by these Presents Constitute and Appoint you to be an Officer in Our Royal Air Force from the* Seventh *day of* July 1955 *. You are therefore carefully and diligently to discharge your Duty as such in the Rank of Pilot Officer or in such other Rank as We may from time to time hereafter be pleased to promote or appoint you to and you are in such manner and on such occasions as may be prescribed by Us to exercise and well discipline in their duties such Officers, Airmen and Airwomen as may be placed under your orders from time to time and use your best endeavours to keep them in good Order and Discipline. And We do hereby Command them to Obey you as their superior Officer and you to Observe and follow such Orders and Directions as from time to time you shall receive from Us, or any superior Officer, according to the Rules and Discipline of War, in pursuance of the Trust hereby reposed in you.*

GIVEN at Our Court, at Saint James's

the Twenty third *day of* August 1955, *in the* Fourth *Year of Our Reign*

By Her Majesty's *Command*

Just as a warrant officer (say, a sergeant-major or a chief petty officer) held the Queen's warrant, so an officer was deemed to hold the Queen's commission, and was entitled to a salute. It was the commission that was being saluted, not the man and not the rank. This was what the actual commission looked like.

CHAPTER 22
MK 1 and MK 2

An officer cadet was expected to be smart and to be good at drill. He was expected to be fit. He was expected to be adept at handling a soldier's weapons. To repeat what the Army repeated constantly: he was expected to be better at all these things than the men he was going to be called upon to lead.

So he spent a lot of time on the parade-ground; he spent a lot of time in the gym and on cross-country runs; he spent a lot of time out on the various weapon ranges and training areas; and of course he spent many an evening in his barrack room bulling his kit.

All this was important. But it was not the whole picture. He spent a lot of time in the classroom too. It was not enough to run, jump, slap a rifle, shine a boot, and hurl a hand grenade. A serving officer, no matter how junior, was expected to *know* something.

So there were lessons every day – lectures, demonstrations, talks – what, today, would be called 'presentations'. But 'presentations' then were rather different from what any class in any subject in any surroundings would expect today. In the 1950s there were no luxuries like overhead projectors, interactive TV screens, computer images, and all the digitised wizardry that any ten-year-old now takes in his stride.

But, primitive equipment or no primitive equipment, that was all they had, and they needed to pay attention. The training programme had an element of inexorability which commanded concentration. Why? Because there were tests to see how much had sunk in. Poor performance could result not in a mere reprimand or a show parade, or even the tiresome 'Restrictions'; bad marks could bring about that most feared punishment in a cadet's life – 'back-squadding'. That is, he would be put back a fortnight or a month in his training, and have to do that intervening set of exercises all over again, with a squad of complete strangers; and all that time he had to witness the progress of his old mates as they made their way to the longed-for passing-out parade. In a sixteen-week course of this intensity, two or four or six weeks could, and did, loom as an eternity.

The ultimate fate, the one talked about in hushed whispers of horror and dread, was RTU. That was being 'Returned to unit'. Expelled. Kicked out. No longer fit to be trained to be an officer. It was even turned into a verb: being 'R.T.U.-ed' meant disappearing right off the screen. Incidentally, you could be R.T.U.-ed for other crimes besides getting 17%; there were all sorts of mortal sins – of commission or omission – outside the classroom that could carry the same dire penalty.

Cadets, then, cajoled their brains to concentrate on subjects that they would never normally have heard of, and not spent a second with even if they had; and they bullied their unwilling memories to remembering the main points of scores of 'Revision notes'. These were pieces of printed foolscap sheets (larger than the universal A4 today), which were given out at the end of nearly every lesson.

At the top, very often, was printed, in capitals, the sinister label 'RESTRICTED'. This meant that the recipient was to treat the material as some kind of military secret that must not, under any circumstances, be communicated to an enemy agent or foreign power. It was difficult to work out how the nation's security was going to be compromised if a cadet told the local spy how many platoons there were in a battalion, or the details of digging slit trenches, but the Army was taking no chances. It is unlikely too that cohorts of shady characters were going to be allowed to haunt the area outside the front gates. And finally, it seemed beyond imagination that any cadet would be so attached to the latest *aide-memoire* on camp hygiene that he would stuff the relevant document inside his battledress blouse when he went out for the evening to the local pub.

But there – he had to listen to a great deal of 'Restricted' information.

About what? About all sorts of things. In no particular order, he had to learn how to send, and receive, wireless signals. Again, a modern soldier would almost cry with laughter at the bulk and primitiveness of the equipment with which his predecessors had to work in the 1950s. The contrast between the bags and boxes and wires and batteries and valves and receivers involved in signalling then, and mobile phones today which enable a child almost anywhere in the world to talk to his grandfather on the other side of that world, are self-evident.

Nevertheless, the cadet had to learn about correct procedure – call signs, sub-stations, corrections and repetitions, message security classification, the signalling alphabet, the difference between 'Roger' and 'Wilco', and a hundred other things. These skills had also be practised.

He had to become acquainted with an encyclopaedia-ful of fresh abbreviations: at random, Coy Comd, MTO, REME, 2IC, Bty Comd, DAQMG, BRASCO, Ord. Rep. Since it was more than likely that the devious enemy might find out what these enigmatic abbreviations might mean, each was also given a CODE NAME, which were known only to the signallers, and which were cleverly designed to hoodwink the aforesaid devious enemy. So a cadet was supposed to learn who (on earth) were SUNRAY, SEAGULL, SHELDRAKE, BLUEBELL, FOXHOUND, MOLAR, ACORN, PRONTO, and so on.

Since Eaton Hall was concerned with training infantry officers, naturally the cadets had to learn all about approach marches, reconnaissance, approaching an enemy position, patrols, attacks both in daylight and at night.

He had to learn the great principle of 'Fire and Movement'; that is, don't commit your entire force (albeit a humble platoon of only twenty-odd men) to a frontal assault. Arrange for part of your command to give covering fire while the rest did the business with the charge against the enemy position.

This may sound simple to an almost infantile degree, but, like so many things when you actually come to do them, it was not quite so easy when you had to do it, for real, out on the ground, with a 'real' enemy (albeit another platoon dressed up as 'the enemy'). A cadet had to be given practice, and experience, in estimating distance, judging the numbers of the enemy, acquiring an eye for ground, learning to spot useful cover, working out how long a certain manoeuvre is likely to take, casting an eye at the weather conditions, knowing how much exertion your men might be capable of after so many hours in the field, and a host of other factors. And of course understanding that military situations have a nasty habit of changing, rapidly, and often.

While all this is going on, of course, there is the platoon commanding officer, a professional, at your shoulder, watching you and judging you, and, when he gets back, giving you so many marks out of ten.

Before you carried out your plan of attack, naturally, you had to decide what the best plan should be. This involved a phenomenon beloved of the Army – what they called a 'military appreciation'. You were required to make a list of 'Courses open to the enemy' (what they could possibly do), and 'Courses open to me' (what I could possibly do). That was only the beginning. That was followed by more lists – advantages of each course open to the enemy, and corresponding disadvantages. And similarly with oneself. It was quite a debate. The cynics would argue that by the time the poor cadet had worked out all this, the battle would have been won or lost. That is as my be, but, as with so many things the Army taught you, it did provide a blueprint, a yardstick, a standard model. The 'appreciation' principle could be, and later was, applicable to so many problems which one might find oneself faced with both in the Army and throughout life. It was not wasted experience.

Fighting a war was not all battles and charges and blood and thunder; there was a lot of static life too – probably, if the truth be told, the vast majority. A cadet had to learn about defence, the dull part. About choosing a defensive position, about digging a trench system, about the placement of the platoon Bren gun and mortar section, fields of fire, sentry rosters, sentry drill, line inspection, barbed wire, making sure that men in the line were regularly visited, fed, and relieved. Again, all common sense, one might say. But it has to be learned, and above all practised. It is not quite as simple as it seems in the Hollywood war films. It is harder still when you are the one who has to issue the orders, and hope that you have not forgotten anything fundamental, especially with that ever-present platoon commander with all the pips on his shoulder watching you.

War was not all attack; it was not all defence either. A great deal of time could be spent in camp or barracks. So there were lectures on fascinating subjects like camp hygiene, sanitation, disease prevention, evacuation of casualties. There were more lectures on what the Army called 'man-management'. The section on 'Morale' had sub-sections on things like 'leadership', 'comradeship', 'discipline', 'self-respect' 'patriotism', 'recognition of service', 'regimental pride'. And on it went. The Army, it seemed, had thought, as it always did, of everything.

Since an officer had to make a lot of things clear to his men, and would be heavily involved in teaching them, he had to learn 'the principles of good instruction'. Once again, it is to the Forces' credit that, though they are often criticised for mindless obedience and obsession with pettifogging detail, they in fact devote so much attention, and attach so much importance, to good teaching, and the teaching of teaching. Compare that attitude with that of many venerable universities – traditionally the home of learning, originality, and clever transmission of ideas – where it was discovered not so long ago that very few of them gave any formal training to their lecturers.

The authorities did not neglect the big picture. A cadet was taught about – and was supposed to remember for his exams – NATO, the Cold War, the danger of nuclear attack. He was supposed to be aware of 'subversive elements in the population' and what to do about them. He was taught about 'Security', alarms, double sentries, road blocks, co-operation with civilian authorities, searching buildings, illuminating search areas after dark, clearing streets, and 'piquetting roof-tops'.

He learned about the organisation of the entire Army. How many platoons in a company; how many companies in a battalion; what Headquarter Company did in a battalion, what rank of officer commanded a division, how the artillery was deployed, what was the difference between a regiment and a corps, what did staff officers do, and so much more.

He was given lessons and drills on co-operating with other branches of the Forces – getting pioneers to develop defences, asking for assistance from specialist groups like three-inch mortar platoons and machine-gun units, bringing down artillery fire on a strong enemy position, calling up air support (a rare luxury, one would imagine, for a humble platoon commander). Nevertheless, it was all there in the training programme.

At least twice in his sixteen weeks, the cadet was required to demonstrate how well all this knowledge had sunk in. The tests were known, unsurprisingly, as 'Military Knowledge One' and 'Military Knowledge Two' – or, in cadet jargon, 'MK 1' and 'MK 2'.

Rather like an execution scheduled for the following morning, it concentrated the mind wonderfully. But if they passed, they could look forward with wary confidence to the final phase of their sixteen weeks, when the end really did begin to show signs of becoming more than a dream. The words 'passing-out parade' came into the conversation.

CHAPTER 23
Officers and Gentlemen

As explained in the previous chapter, it was not enough for an officer cadet to learn how to do drill better than his men, or to be fitter than his men, or to be more adept at weapon-handling; he had to learn a lot too. Sheer knowledge.

That was not enough either. He had to be taught how to put all this knowledge into practice, and he had to be seen performing it. That meant outdoors, on the ground, sometimes literally 'on the ground'. He did training in organising and carrying out patrols, both in daylight and at night. He had to effect a raid on an enemy trench and bring away a 'captive'. He did long marches and night guards; he dug trenches; he crawled over rough ground with live ammunition whizzing a (hopefully) safe distance above his head. He spent whole days (and nights) out of doors practising many of these skills – and many more. As always, there were the ubiquitous platoon commanders hovering somewhere close by, watching and judging every move.

A further incentive was the business of rewards for the best cadets. From each fortnightly intake the platoon commanders, in conjunction with the company commander (a major), would select three or four of the cadets they judged the best, or at any rate the most promising; these fortunate young men were to be designated 'Junior Under-Officers' – or 'JUO's'. From this elite band would be chosen the 'best of the best' – to be known as the 'Senior Under-Officer' – predictably 'SUO'. They were given a special device to be sewn on the lower part of their sleeve.

Round about the same time, all three platoons were packed off to 'Battle Camp'. This lasted a fortnight, and took up the thirteenth and fourteenth weeks of the four months. Fortunately it did mean permanent accommodation, except of course for some of the exercises. The Army's use of the word 'camp' did not, mercifully, refer exclusively to tents and mud-soaked communal toilets. The barrack rooms were, by military standards, quite good. The food was very good. Even more of a blessing, the Army had laid on constant, reliable, *hot* baths and showers. And they were certainly needed. There was even a large, and very effective, drying room provided for mud- and rain-soaked kit and clothing. So nobody could complain that he had not enough facilities to enable him to recover from his exertions.

And exertions there most certainly were, day after day.

There were platoon attacks, company attacks, uphill, downhill, across country. There were withdrawals. Mortars were fired. Smoke screens were laid. The by now notorious 'Fire and Movement' manoeuvre was practised, endlessly. All-round defence was organised, and, of course, judged and assessed. Everybody got used to seeing tracer ammunition fired. This was quite exciting, to see the white shafts whizzing away like Jovian thunderbolts. It proved to the human eye that bullets did not go straight; they rose and fell, they had a trajectory.

They did not fire it themselves, of course. That was done by professionals, regulars. With medium machine-guns. Most impressive firearms, they were. Water-cooled – could fire all day if properly maintained. More than impressive; they were awe-inspiring. Everyone knew that it was weapons like these which had inflicted the horrors of the Western Front in the Great War.

It was the regulars too who fired live rounds over the cadets' heads while they were scrambling through heather or sphagnum moss towards their objective. If cadets had never heard of sphagnum moss before they joined the Army, two weeks at battle camp etched the memory of it on the brain for life.

Battle camp took place in North Wales, conveniently not too distant from Chester and Eaton Hall. Cadets' memory of it was pretty universally grey, because of the endless slate roofs of the nearby houses, the quarries, the grubbiness of the millions of sheep, the smoke-stained railways, and the all-penetrating rain. It being North Wales, there was no shortage of hills and mountains, many of them covered by endless heath and heather. So far so good – at least tolerable.

The trouble was that the area had also been used for practice in the firing of three-inch mortars. When these shells landed, they naturally exploded, and blew the surrounding vegetation and earth all over the place. The resultant hole went down for, say, two or three feet, till one came to the underlying rock. As the months passed after the explosions, sphagnum grew to fill the hole, with its characteristic sickly green crust. To the untrained eye, and also from a distance, it looked solid.

Cadets consumed by a company withdrawal, with lungs bursting from lugging a Bren gun half a mile up his and down dale, were not as watchful or as circumspect as they should have been. It was a rare cadet who had not, at some time, had the infuriating experience of plunging without warning into three feet of bog – and having to continue for the rest of the day, soaked to the crotch or even the waist.

Once Battle Camp was behind them, the cadets could look forward to their last two weeks being housed in the Hall itself, and of course to the growing light at the end of the tunnel.

But the learning was not over yet – not by a long chalk. They were introduced to the legal complexities of a court of inquiry. They were shown how 'company orders' was organised. (This was the trial and punishment session that a company commander was required to conduct regularly. He was empowered to impose a certain range of penalties, unless the defendant elected to go before the Commanding Officer.) They had to learn how to give evidence, what evidence was admissible, and so on.

They were inducted into the mysteries of 'Battlecraft' and 'Fieldcraft'. Map-reading skills continued to be regularly tested. They found out what intelligence officers did. Even more of a mystery, they found out what staff officers did. They were taught about 'Relief in the Line'. They were even taught minelaying, and, rather more dangerous, mine-lifting. Luckily, there were no practical lessons devoted to this.

Rather more relevant, they were taught 'The Principles of War'. There was not time to try and turn them into clones of Frederick the Great or von Clausewitz, but at least they were introduced to matters like Security, Surprise, Concentration of Effort, Economy of Effort, Flexibility, Sound Administration. One might argue that a few minutes' deep thought ought to produce the same conclusions. Maybe so, in the comfort of a venerable armchair. These were young men, extremely well-occupied young men, young men who were not by definition dedicated to the God of War. Frankly not very knowledgeable young men. They needed constant direction. The Army was very good at giving them that.

The Army was also very good at showing the full picture. They had even thought ahead. It was not enough to put a pip on a young soldier's shoulder and turn him loose. He had to be prepared for an officer's life.

Yet more lectures were given, and foolscap 'Revision Notes' and 'Students' Precis' provided to keep and to study. A new young officer did not just walk into his first officers' mess and take it from there. He had to learn 'General Military Etiquette'. When to salute a major in your own regiment and when not to. How to address the Commanding Officer – is it 'Colonel' or is it simply 'Sir'? When to wear uniform off duty and when not to. Hats are to be worn when out in the street, even in civilian clothes. The story was current that

Guards officers were not to be seen carrying a parcel when in civilian clothes, never mind when in uniform.

But then the Guards were, as mentioned before, a law unto themselves. There was a whole section of notes on what to do if you were commissioned into the Guards. You were warned that 'dinner customs vary considerably within the Brigade'. So God help you if you go into the Mess at the Coldstream Guards and do it the Grenadier Guards way. There were pitfalls *outside* the Officers' Mess too. For instance, a Guards officer needed to know that 'all full corporals hold the appointment of Lance-Sergeant and are members of the Sergeants' Mess'. Regimental Sergeant-Majors are to be addressed as 'Sergeant-Major' and *never* as 'Mr'. Trust the Guards to be different.

It was the same with the line regiments. Do you wear your Sam Browne belt when you enter the Mess or do you take it off? Or do you take it off only when you enter the dining room? On regimental guest nights make sure you proceed into the dining room in strict order of precedence. Don't smoke until the Commanding Officer gives permission.

And so it went on. Don't talk shop in the Mess. Don't talk politics or religion. Don't criticise Mess staff; complain to a member of the Mess Committee. If you are invited to the Sergeants' Mess, 'NEVER get drunk' there.

Make yourself familiar with the traditions and customs of the regiment in which you find yourself commissioned. Understand the origins of the cap badge; memorise the regiment's battle honours and how they were won; know what the regiment's nickname is. There were scores of them. For instance, the Royal Scots were known as 'Pontius Pilate's Bodyguard'. The Devonshire Regiment (the old 11th of Foot) was known as 'The Bloody Eleventh', after its 75% casualties at the Battle of Salamanca in 1812.

This assumed, of course, that a cadet knew the regiment into which he was about to be commissioned. He was required to make a choice – three choices actually, in descending order of desire. He was usually given an interview while at Eaton Hall by an officer from the regiments of his choices, and he could only hope that one of those three interviews would be successful.

Meanwhile the end loomed nearer. That meant the passing-out parade.

A book like this could print endless photographs of these events, and they would nearly all be the same. Tens of thousands of officer cadets passed through the gates of Eaton Hall during the fifteen years of National Service. Roughly a third of that number also did National Service in the RAF. That was more passing-out parades. The Navy took only a few per cent of national servicemen, but there still must have been quite a few hundred parades over the years. There was also the small matter of the rest of the two and half million who did not attend officer cadet school, but who still had their own passing-out parade at the end of basic training. That was an awful lot of passing-out parades.

Nevertheless, to the individual officer cadet coming to the end of probably the most intense sixteen weeks of his life, the passing-out parade, *his* passing-out parade, was of enormous importance. He had been in the Army long enough now to get a glimmering of what it was all about. He had come through a huge number of tests of every possible kind. Understandably he wanted to show off just a little about it. He knew that his family would be coming to watch the event. He knew that his drill instructors wanted to make a good show as well; he now understood something about their feelings and motivation. He knew they were all working together. Even that automaton the RSM, though nobody really knew about him.

Rehearsals were numerous and onerous. A break-through came about the middle of the final week, when the band appeared, and played for the marching. If one has never marched to a military band, one can have no idea of the colossal lift to the morale a band can give. Suddenly they all felt a million dollars.

So the parade came, and went. They were now officers. But that of course was just the beginning.

CHAPTER 24
For Real

On the edge of the town of Bayeux in Normandy is a cemetery – a war cemetery. It contains the graves of some of the thousands of servicemen who died in the D-Day landings in June, 1944 – what their French hosts (and beneficiaries) call the '*Débarquement*'. It is like the dozens, possibly scores, of other war cemeteries scattered all over northern and eastern France, and Belgium, containing the remains of the dead from two World Wars. (Germany too – death showed no preference.)

All war cemeteries are by definition sad places, but what gives particular poignancy to the one at Bayeux is the fact that each grave gives not only the name, but also the age, of the dead man beneath – 18, 20, 22, 17, 18, 17, 19, 17 – and so on. So, so young.

The National Service Act had decreed that the male youth of Britain was eligible for call-up from the age of seventeen. As explained in previous chapters, many managed to have their call-up deferred – to eighteen, to twenty-one, even beyond. But many too found themselves in uniform before their eighteenth birthday – the same age as so many of the soldiers, sailors, and airmen whose remains fill all those war cemeteries.

But nothing to worry about, one might have thought; the War was over. Hitler was dead; the world was at peace. The victors had founded the United Nations to police the world. The worst a young soldier could fear then was a spot of sentry duty round the arms store.

Not so.

That decade and a half were to see, if not countless, certainly distressingly many, local wars, rumours of wars, threats of wars, and – dear God! – dark clouds of a possible *Third World War*.

For instance, there was a civil war in Greece in 1946, in which the British Government was involved in order to prevent the country being taken over by the Communists, who were backed by Josef Stalin.

In 1947, there was potential trouble on a cataclysmic scale over the issue of Indian independence and the relative demands and mutual hatreds of hundreds of millions of Hindus and Moslems. India was part of the British Empire.

In Palestine, which had been administered by the British since the end of the First World War, there had been a promise given to setting up the Jewish state of Israel, to which most of its Arab neighbours were bitterly opposed. Israel was indeed proclaimed in 1948, and the British had formally left Palestine by that time, but war broke out in 1949. By this time one of the chief preoccupations of the Government was maintenance of oil supplies from the Arab countries, so a very difficult balancing act was required – to try and keep face by supporting the Israelis without driving the Arabs into military opposition.

It got worse. In 1949 the Communist leader Mao Tse-tung set up a dictatorship in China, so the British possession of Hong Kong came under threat. Worse still, Communist influence and political power were threatening to spread right across south-eastern Asia.

It wasn't much better closer to home. In Winston Churchill's famous phrase, an 'iron curtain' had descended upon the whole of eastern Europe after the War, and Communist dictatorships were set up, with backing from the Kremlin, in Poland, Latvia, Lithuania, Estonia, Czechoslovakia, Hungary, Rumania, Bulgaria, Albania, and Yugoslavia.

(Yugoslavia soon broke away from Russian domination, but it remained a 'closed' country, and a Communist one.)

Germany was split into two – the western half soon to become a western-style democracy and the eastern half to be known as a 'People's Republic' – in other words a Russian-dominated dictatorship. This tension was screwed up infinitely higher when the Russians closed the roads to Berlin. The western half of Berlin was run by the western allies, and it looked as if the whole city would now fall under Communist rule. The peace of Europe teetered on a knife edge.

In all of these situations, understandably, the British armed forces had to be ready to be deployed. In fact, for the most part, they were not. But as far as national servicemen were concerned, they could be, at any moment. It is easy to be complacent with the confidence of hindsight, but it did not seem like nothing to worry about when you were actually living through it – in an Army barracks on Salisbury Plain or in a huge NATO complex somewhere in the middle of Germany. The whole NATO concept was founded on the distinct likelihood of a Russian invasion of Western Europe. That meant that troops had to be ready – to meet any kind of attack, both nuclear and 'conventional' (the current euphemism for the old-fashioned 'Second-World-War' style of fighting).

National Service had been conceived as a way of filling Britain's military obligations when the conscripts who had been called up for service in the War had been demobbed and sent home. So if these young men did not find themselves actually fighting a war, they often found themselves facing the possibility of one, or of being kept at various levels of readiness somewhere near to one.

In 1950 the possibility became a fact. The Communists of North Korea invaded the western-style democracy of South Korea. Peace in the Pacific was vital to the USA. The Pacific was the most important feature of their entire eastern security system. Moreover they were implacably opposed to Communism, and to dictatorships. They had no choice but to intervene. Britain was America's closest ally. If Korea fell, Hong Kong could be next, and south-east Asia was already under threat. The United Nations had been recently founded to protect the world from such aggression. Again, there seemed to be no choice.

This time, then, it was the real thing. Actual fighting would have to be done, and done by, among others, national servicemen. There were some qualms about sending seventeen-year-olds to do it, so these young men were stationed in Hong Kong until they reached their eighteenth birthday. Which of course made all the difference. They were now deemed *much* more able to cope with thousands of North Korean soldiers, and hundreds of thousands of Chinese 'volunteers', who had gallantly chosen to support their Communist brothers in their crusade against the enemies of Karl Marx.

In the event, many of these national servicemen did cope very well. They served alongside regulars in the various infantry regiments, artillery and support units – the Service Corps, the Ordnance Corps, the Medical Corps, the Royal Engineers, the Signals Corps, the Pioneer Corps, and a host of other specialist organisations.

All wars are awful, and the Korean War was no exception. But at least it was 'out in the open'. There were battlefields. There were traditional campaigns. That did not make it any more bearable; it was just that a soldier could understand it. It fitted his idea of war. It was the sort of war he had been trained to fight.

Unfortunately, the 1950s were to bring along other types of fighting that made it necessary to re-think the whole business of fighting from the ground up. In Malaya (now Malaysia) the trouble had in fact begun before 1950, but had been upstaged by the Korean conflict. As the decade advanced, the activities of the Malayan National Liberation Army gradually sucked in up to 40,000 British troops to deal with them, as well as men from the King's African Rifles and the Gurkhas, and from Australia and New Zealand.

National servicemen were there too, and showed their versatility and flexibility by putting to good use the lessons they had learned at the Jungle Warfare School. They had a share in putting down the insurgency, for all that it took until 1960. Nevertheless, they must have taken some satisfaction from the fact that they had succeeded in suppressing a communist insurgency, whereas, in Vietnam, the Americans failed. (There are many reasons for this, and this book is not the place to go into them.)

Yet another type of warfare had to be learnt in Kenya. Here the authorities had to deal with an insurgency that had all sorts of overtones – political, economic, religious, tribal. It constituted a threat to security which absorbed several military units, both British and African, from 1952 onwards. The back of the revolt was broken by 1956, but embers continued to glow until about 1960. National Servicemen were once again involved, and learned all sorts of new skills to enable them to deal with the terrain, the climate, and the nature of the people they were fighting.

A similar situation arose in Cyprus round about the same time. The British, who had gained a protectorate over Cyprus in the 1870s, found themselves embroiled in a dispute between the Turkish and Greek elements of the population. This was particularly embarrassing, because the Government used Cyprus as a vital military base in the Eastern Mediterranean. The importance of Cyprus to this policy became even greater when Britain was forced out of Egypt after the Suez debacle. The peace was broken by the activities of Greek insurgents, who wanted Cyprus to be united with Greece. Yet more national servicemen served in the cause of security and terrorist-hunting.

Perhaps the most controversial campaign that involved national servicemen was the ill-fated, and short-lived enterprise around Suez and the Canal. When the newly-arrived Egyptian leader Nasser announced the nationalisation of the Suez Canal, once again the British Government felt that it had to respond. Ever since its opening in 1869, the Canal had been the main artery of communication for the British Empire. After the War, with the Indian dimension of the Empire gone, Suez remained vital because of its indispensability for the transporting of Middle East oil to the West. And because of the Cold War between the Soviet Union and the West, it would also be equally vital for the movement of troops from Australia and New Zealand in case they were needed to combat an invasion of Europe by the ever-threatening Russians.

The pressure was even greater on Anthony Eden, the British Prime Minister, because he had been Foreign Secretary during the 1930s, when Hitler was constantly calling Europe's bluff with his relentless territorial demands. Eden was convinced that Nasser was another Hitler in this matter, and that he had to be stopped. The French thought the same. So, for even more urgent reasons, did the Israelis, who lived in a constant state of semi-siege from the surrounding, and very ill-disposed, Arab nations.

Rightly or wrongly, Eden, the French, and the Israelis invaded in late 1956 in order to 'rescue' the Canal from Nasser's clutches. The Russians were opposed, naturally. More frustratingly, so were the Americans. The pressure on Eden was too great. By the end of the year, the invading forces had been recalled. The issue had split Britain from top to bottom. Was Eden trying bravely to face down a posturing bully, or was he engaged in a pitiful attempt to behave as if Britannia still ruled the waves? Whatever the final result, national servicemen had been involved yet again.

Hong Kong, Korea, Kenya, Cyprus, Malaya, Suez, the NATO defence of Western Europe – it was a pretty fair roster, if not of battle honours, at least of potential or actual battle involvement, for a generation of young men who, if they had had their way, would have had nothing to do with the military life. It is a fine testimony to the skill and professionalism of those regulars who were charged with training them that they were considered fit to be sent to all those places.

It says a great deal for the resilience and adaptability of those same young men. It says a great deal too for their bravery. Nearly four hundred of them died.

FOREIGN LIFE

In an institution which involved over two million men, it is of course impossible to illustrate the whole range of sights, conditions, and circumstances that awaited them after their basic training. The most one can hope for is to point out just a few of the surprises, contrasts, challenges, and new experiences that these young men had to meet. As a wider range of these features arose during service abroad, most of the photographs which follow are taken from that service. Just about a half of all national servicemen went abroad somewhere or other. And most photos from abroad are more interesting than those taken at home.

No author can describe what everyone had to face, but by describing one set of circumstances, one hopes that veterans reading about them will have their own memories revived about what they did.

Look at this daunting pile – almost like a United Nations building. In fact it was the headquarters of the 2nd Tactical Air Force in Germany in the mid-1950s. All ready to deal with the beastly Russians.

If on the other hand, you were posted to East Africa, this was the main road which took you north from Nairobi.

And this was the road which took you from one half of the battalion to the other. Quite a highway. Ready to deal with all emergencies.

This was the sort of township you would meet in Equatorial Africa. It was called Nanyuki. Its appearance conjures up memories of hundreds of frontier towns in Hollywood westerns, with perhaps just a touch of Sanders of the River *as well.*

Far-away places – huge mountains, heathland not very far removed from that in England, a river which could have come straight out of Exmoor. No trackless jungle. Very often, the surprise came not from what was there, but from what wasn't.

Mt. Kenya itself sometimes wasn't there, hidden behind the daily rain – almost set your clock by it.

EVERYDAY SERVICE LIFE

Service in Germany seemed to have the edge on service elsewhere. Perhaps it was American money propping up NATO. Look at these facilities, admittedly for officers. But at least all the buildings – for everybody – were permanent.

Compare the German accommodation with that on display here in Africa – and this was for everybody – other ranks, officers, and all. For months on end.

Again, compare the officers' mess in Germany with the virtual shack here. Yet mess waiters were dressed like something out of an empire-builders' annual. Log cabin and Savoy service – a curious mixture.

Alas, the kitchen could not boast Savoy facilities. Certainly not washing-up machines. The cook was a Jekyll and Hyde figure – in kitchen gear he could have come out of the seediest dive east of Suez; in walking-out kit, he was a credit to any army.

This construction saw to the sanitary demands of dozens of men – of all ranks. Apparently 'it is a truth universally acknowledged' (well, it was in military medical circles) that if you dig a hole deep enough, it never fills up – with whatever organic material you drop into it. It will, I am sure, be a commonplace to all chemists and biologists.

PERSONAL ACCOMODATION

Compare this junior officers' accommodation with ...

... the subalterns' lines in a battalion in East Africa.

When you had been
there long enough to
learn the ropes, it was
possible to hire a
couple of askaris to
build a wall of
bamboo, and perch the
canvas on top of it, so
doubling the space
inside. They had
obviously done it
scores of times, and
had learned
techniques with
bamboo and machete
from the cradle. It
only took them a day.

If you were there long enough, you branched out into gardening and flower beds – the passion to re-create a little spot of England…

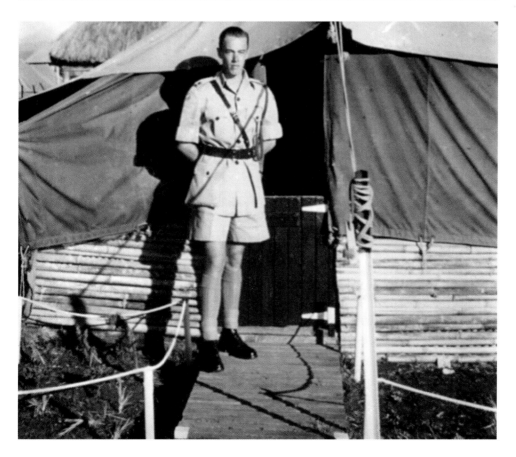

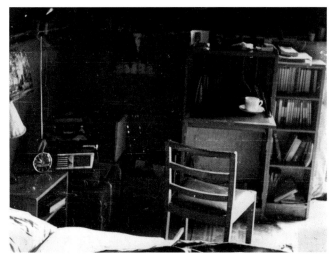

With duckboards, sacking for wallpaper, and some imaginative furniture arrangements, it was surprising what could be done. Of necessity; it might have to be home for six months or a year.

WORK

Postings abroad usually involved some serious soldiering.

For example, when it came to mopping up the last traces of the Mau-Mau terrorists in Kenya, who had taken refuge in the surrounding forest, officers and NCOs were sent on a tracking course.

It sounded something like the Boy Scouts, but it was not quite as simple as that. The askari trackers, who laid the trail for the European pupils to follow, often raised their eyes Heavenwards at the inability of these supposedly intelligent Europeans to follow the most obvious tell-tale signs.

Chasing desperate outlaws in the forest was no joke. Quite apart from the vegetation, the weather, and the difficulty of tracking, there was always the danger of ambush.

TRANSPORT AND MUD

The Land Rover appeared in 1947. It became so universal that one wonders what the Army did before. Similarly, the ubiquitous three-tonner will be instantly familiar to everybody who has done any kind of military service anywhere.

The transport section boasted its own signwriter. Note the machete in the askari's hand. The universal instrument/weapon, as, sadly, the Mau-Mau were to demonstrate in their raids.

It is so easy to take roads for granted. If there aren't any, weather conditions suddenly loom very large. It can become a feat just getting there.

CHAPTER 25
Holding up the Empire

Anybody who embarks on writing about National Service, especially one who actually remembers doing it, soon comes across the problem of explanation. Words, phrases, concepts, names which he has always taken for granted are no longer universally known or accepted. For example, a whole generation has grown up knowing nothing of the Cold War, the Berlin Wall, the Politburo, Nationalist China, BAOR, Mr Molotov, King Farouk, sputniks, bombs on Bikini Atoll, the LNER, and Gorgeous Gussie. There are scores of others – universally known in the decade following the War, but needing to be included in a glossary today.

So one mentions 'the British Empire' with some hesitancy. First because it is largely not there any more – not in the form in which national servicemen grew up to know. Second because it came in for so much criticism from left-wing politicians and colonial liberation movements that an ordinary Englishman was brought almost to the state of feeling ashamed of it. Thirdly, much fresh information has come to light because the passage of time has allowed the release of 'sensitive' documents, most of which do not seem to reflect much credit on the relevant imperial authorities. And fourthly, the period covered by National Service coincided closely with the fragmentation of that very 'Empire', during which one region after another emerged from 'exploitation' or 'servitude' or mere 'domination' according to the taste of the polemical journalists and propagandists involved; adopted as often as not a new name; brandished a multicoloured new national flag; and was duly received into the United Nations.

It is a moot point: did colonial independence movements thrive because the Empire was having such a bad press and was therefore less resistant to change, or was the Empire having a bad press because so many colonial independence movements were so successful, and so vociferous about the evils of imperialism?

Whatever the truth of the matter, the fact remains that during that time British Armed Forces were quite extensively involved with many of those areas coloured pink on the world map. And if British Armed Forces were so involved, it followed that a percentage of those forces would be made up of national servicemen.

Some of those postings would have been regarded as highly desirable, such as Bermuda – miles away from anywhere in the Atlantic, no threats from the nasty Russians, no noisy liberation movements, a smashing climate, and very little to do.

The same might have been said for Jamaica, the public perception of which amounted to an amalgam of sun, sand, rum, and calypso. The multi-racial reality was not quite so idyllic.

It was certainly not idyllic with one particular paradise spot – Christmas Island in the Pacific. Or supposed paradise spot. Some national servicemen were on hand to witness the explosion of Britain's first thermonuclear device, in 1957. Some of them were to suffer a lifetime of unexplained illnesses, and were to become involved in decades of unresolved litigation to try and gain some compensation.

The commonest 'imperial' posting was to somewhere in Africa. Names that were well known then – Tanganyika, Nyasaland, Rhodesia, the Gold Coast – have been replaced by fresh identities like Tanzania, Malawi, Zambia, Zimbabwe, Ghana (often not new names, but names reflecting much older, pre-colonial history). Kenya *looks* the same, but is in fact different. In 'imperial' times it was customary for Europeans to pronounce it with a long 'e', as in 'Keenya'. Now of course it is pronounced the way of the Swahili language – 'Kenya'.

What follows is a stylised account of the sort of thing that a national serviceman could expect if he were to be posted to one or other of these countries. Veterans who actually experienced it will naturally take issue with the detail, but the author hopes and trusts that there will be many features of his description which will be common to the lives of them all.

Once he had been told of his destination, the next thing he heard (and it did not necessarily follow quickly) was detailed instructions about where to report – an 'assembly centre' or a 'trooping unit', probably somewhere in London, when he would be transported to a suitably accessible airfield. Note 'airfield', not 'airport'. None of your passenger lounges at Gatwick or Heathrow.

None of your air-conditioned jumbo jets either. Turbo-prop was the norm. Functional cinema-style seats with the screws still visible holding them to the floor. No cabin crew either. In contrast with a modern holiday flight which can take you almost anywhere in Western Europe in about two hours or less, the flight to Malta took five hours. And that was only the first leg.

You had to begin to get used to the heat while still in the heavy battledress which was universal wear in England. There was a scratch meal available, and you boarded another turbo-prop Viking for the next leg – to Benghazi in Libya, or, if you were unlucky, to Khartoum in the Sudan. By this time it was probably dark, which was a good thing, because Benghazi in battledress could be tropical; Khartoum could be infernal.

With luck you reached your destination airport late in the following afternoon, after a journey of over thirty hours. (Compare it with today, when you can fly, non-stop, from London to Australia in about eighteen.) But please note, destination 'airport'. You were not there yet. Africa was a big place; individual countries were big places. The chances were that you had a hundred-mile journey in front of you, in the back of a three-ton Army truck, along roads which were largely unmetalled.

You arrived late, and were given, if you were lucky, a mattress or camp bed in some bare room or other, perhaps only a tent. And you took it from there.

Who were you, by the way? You might be a fresh-faced, newly-trained NS subaltern, full of what you had learned at Eaton Hall. One glance the next morning at the weather, the hundreds of tents around you, the log shack of an officers' mess, the assortment of black and brown faces gazing curiously; one syllable of a foreign language (possibly several foreign languages) – and you would be wondering what on earth was the use of anything that you had been taught there.

You might, on the other hand, be some kind of a specialist – a mechanic in REME (Royal Electrical and Mechanical Engineers), a signaller in, obviously, the Royal Corps of Signals. You could be in one of the various corps – the Royal Army Service Corps, or the Royal Army Ordnance Corps. If your unit was engaged in work in the nearby forest tracking criminals or terrorists, you could be a dog-handler. If you had missed selection for officer training, but could boast a clutch of 'O' Levels or 'A' Levels, you could be a sergeant in the Education Corps.

If you were a national service officer with the right qualifications from civilian life, you could be, not a subaltern, but a captain – a regimental Medical Officer or a battalion Paymaster. If the local military situation demanded it, you could be an Intelligence Officer.

Whoever you were, you were all equal in what you had to learn next – how to get used to 'tropical kit' – bush jackets and baggy empire-builder shorts; scrounging enough furniture and fittings from the Quartermaster to make a tent or a small room habitable; finding your way round a town barracks or a huge tented camp on the edge of the 'bush' or whatever the locals called it; making the acquaintance of the Commanding Officer, the Adjutant, the

Quartermaster (as already indicated – a most indispensable gentleman), the Regimental Sergeant-Major; and finding out what and where the eating facilities were.

Above all, you had to take your first steps in learning the language. There might be a regional *lingua franca*, as in East Africa – Swahili. All the African troops spoke it; many of them had to learn it too, because where they came from everybody had spoken only the local tribal language. There might be four, five, six tribal languages in any one unit, but mercifully you weren't expected to learn those.

A second mercy was that you were not expected to learn even the *lingua franca* to any kind of great grammatical ceiling. A few score vital nouns; some necessary Army verbs (and it didn't matter much if you mangled the verb endings); some indispensable prepositions and adverbs like 'left' and 'right', 'up' and 'down', 'slowly' and 'quickly'; and you were in business. If you did aspire to gaining a better command (and you were encouraged to), there was an exam you could take. If you passed (it was about the equivalent to the old 'O' Level), you were given an extra four shillings a day's pay – 20p. Still worth having – then.

However tenuous your eventual grasp of the lingo, that, coupled with your day-to-day work with African troops, would prove to be a sort of second education. Few national servicemen had travelled beyond the borders of the United Kingdom. Most civilian wages were not princely. The Government's post-war austerity policy decreed that you were not allowed to spend much abroad anyway. In the very early days it was £25 – for a year. Even for the late 1940s that was low. The great airborne holiday boom had not got under way. Television documentaries had not appeared to whet the travel appetite.

Hence, the opportunity to travel to places like Africa was, for most young men, unique. And being young, they were correspondingly impressed. They were perhaps slightly bemused too, because of the perks involved. There were 'foreign allowances' added to weekly pay. Duties on things like alcohol and cigarettes were mouth-wateringly low – fifty cigarettes for the equivalent of 10p. Labour was cheap. Officers could hire civilian valets for 50p. a week. Local Asian shopkeepers and tailors could offer a wide range of goods and bespoke clothing for, again, absurd prices. In a military establishment, all sorts of wheezes could be cooked up to provide oneself with the means of travel – coupling trips for sport or sight-seeing with military errands in military vehicles – and therefore free. Money could be saved for an adventurous two weeks' leave in a variety of exotic tropical resorts. There were whole menageries of wild animals to be filmed – in their own habitats. It was all great fun.

There was work to be done, of course. If there was a local emergency or any kind of security threat, that could involve exertion, some hardship, and occasionally danger – if not from the local nasties, then from the local wildlife. Generally speaking, if you used your common sense, obeyed unit standing orders, and didn't do anything stupid, you were safe. When rare incidents occurred of young servicemen coming to grief (over-reported in the domestic press without the boring background details about standing orders), it was, as often as not, because those standing orders had been ignored.

There was a whole new world to be learnt about: dealing with African soldiers; learning about their tribal background; gaining an insight into their nation's history; getting a tiny toehold on national politics; watching, and not always approving of, the attitudes of those Europeans who had lived there for years.

However, for all that it was new, and exciting, and absorbing, the fact remained that it was a long way from home. There were no e-mails; there were no mobile phones; no i-pods, no i-pads, no videos, no CDs. The best you could hope for was a weekly 'cinema' show in a NAAFI hut where the projectionist operated in a jungle of reels and broken fuses and sagging yards of 8mm film.

So you still counted the days to 'demob.'

There was one consolation, if indeed you counted it as consolation. If you were in an area of an officially-declared 'Emergency', and you were there for ninety days, you qualified for a campaign medal. Not much, to be sure, but the ribbon looked good.

CHAPTER 26
Falling on Your Feet

In a period of about fifteen or sixteen years, something like two and a half million young men went through the experience of National Service. There was never, apparently, any question of submitting young women to the same fate. They had been needed during the War all right. After the War, the Government had taken the controversial step of renewing conscription in order to fulfil the many remaining commitments of the Armed Forces all over the world, but, suddenly, it seemed, those commitments did not involve women any more. Perhaps the Cabinet decided that the electorate just wouldn't wear it. Calling up the young *men* had enough opponents as it was – even within the Labour party, the party of government. Calling up the future wives of all those returning war veterans would have probably been electoral suicide.

It was certainly controversial for those two and half million young men. To all of them it was a novelty. For most of them it was a shock – at any rate the first dozen or so weeks of basic training. Most of them too found at the end of it all that it had certainly been an experience. Some freely admitted that it had been a most useful experience. Others claimed bitterly that, after the first twelve weeks, it had been one long bore. And, by the law of averages, there must have some for whom it was hell. By the same law of averages, there were some who declared that it had been a breeze.

Wherein lies the truth? The chances are – everywhere.

In any group as large as the one under discussion, there must have some who had a very unpleasant time – either because of repetitious, boring, unsavoury work, or because of unfair treatment, or, obviously, because of the trauma of active service. So there was a predictable percentage of permanent sanitary orderlies, pen-pushers, kitchen cleaners, nervous wrecks, and cripples. Very sad. And it should not have happened.

But in that same large group, there is always a percentage of those who enjoy more than their fair share of quick wits, good connections, opportunism, and luck. The ones who always come up smelling of roses.

The stories of their good fortune were the stuff of barrack room gossip and anecdote, and, while the audience, in their mid-training slough of despond amid the blanco and the shoe polish, were prey to the natural mixture of envy and wishful thinking, their common sense told them that not all these stories could be right. The world just wasn't like that.

Be that as it may, the stories went the rounds. They could be transparently apocryphal; they could be highly selective; they could be embellished; they could be economical with the truth; they could be impossible; and they could be plain untrue. Good listening though.

Like the one about the soldier who tried to escape bulling by giving his boots a perfect, and permanent, shine; he painted the toecaps with nail varnish. Constant applications produced a beautiful but brittle shell, which, one day, under the stress of the regular stamping, caused the entire toecap carapace to fly off in a detonation of shards, leaving its host leather beneath as a shrivelled pock-marked corpse (like the young girl who tried to escape from Shangri-La, and who turned into a wizened crone in hours). A further, dramatic, twist would be given by the addition of the dramatically ironic detail that the incident occurred when the wearer was in front of the Commanding Officer's desk – on CO's orders for congratulation on the high standard of his boots.

Then there was the story of the resourceful conscript who tried to pretend that he was educationally sub-normal. He achieved this, apparently, by managing to fail the basic intelligence tests – quite a feat. He was half-way, he thought, to being released. But no. The fringe details included the conscript being given a choice: would he like to be given a shilling (5p.) or half a crown (12½p.). If he chose the half-crown, he clearly wasn't as stupid as all that, so away he went to basic training; if he chose the shilling, he was hauled off to classes with the Education Corps and taught basic arithmetic. You never won with the Army.

There was one young man of the author's acquaintance, however, who actually made it by means of deficiencies in his health. And without trying. He had a calling, he said, for the ministry, but wanted to do his two years first because he thought it would give him more knowledge of Life, and so make him a better shepherd of his future flock. But within a few days he came out in a most unpleasant rash, all over his face and arms. Off to the Medical Officer. Off again to a distant specialist hospital for 'tests'. Back came the verdict: he was allergic to blanco. Quite unsuitable then for soldiering. He was invalided out before he had done a fortnight. He was inconsolable. Now he would never learn about Life before he went into theological college.

Several stories were based on the old chestnut that what matters is not what you know but who you know (or 'whom' for the purists). So the average anecdote went something like this: a certain young guardsman with a double-barrelled name, late of some swish, double-barrelled public school, didn't have two 'O' Levels to rub together, but he had an uncle who was a colonel attached to the Imperial General Staff; so he wound up with a desk job at the War Office, and he never even had to wear uniform. Lucky lad.

It might on the other hand be pure chance. The author had the good fortune to be sent for interview before a bemedalled general, who just happened to be the Colonel-in-Chief of a regiment into which he had asked to be commissioned. He had requested secondment from that regiment to a posting abroad. He got it.

Escape figured largely in another cycle of yarns. This school of thought clearly worked on the principle of sideways thinking. It was a wearisome procedure to exhaust the imagination trying to dream up ways of outwitting the authorities; far better to work out how to avoid the authorities altogether. Just make sure that you were not there. In other words, leave the country. Emigration was a little radical, and tended to be rather permanent. Once you were there, you might have to stay. World travel was difficult – no bargain jet flights to help you keep occasional contact with your family, and no satellite phone to keep daily contact with them.

If long-distance escape looked too drastic, there was always the Channel Islands. A loophole, or an anomaly, in the law allowed islanders to remain exempt from National Service. And there was no restriction known to the author about staying there. It was British territory, just like any county away from your home. Like going to live in Fermanagh or Fife.

The trouble was the smaller print in the National Service Act: you were deemed eligible for call-up until you were twenty-six. So – Jersey or Johannesburg, Guernsey or Gambia – you had to steel yourself for eight or nine years away. If you came back before the time was up, 'they' could get you. The Military Police could be knocking on your door and inviting you to go with them. If you popped back simply in order to arrange a transfer from one foreign university to another, in order to embark on yet another degree course, 'they' could get you again. So it was a demanding strategy you had imposed on yourself.

Sometimes it was pure Fate, and had nothing to do with quick wits or sideways thinking. Reference has already been made to postings to Bermuda, which admittedly were not exactly numerous. No hard evidence has been forthcoming about what one actually did in Bermuda, but it is difficult to imagine how a posting there could bear any resemblance to Devil's Island.

You did not necessarily have to be an officer to get a soft spot. A big allied headquarters in, say, Fontainebleau needed drivers just as any other unit did – probably more. What else could the poor fellows do in off-duty hours but pine away in Paris? Later postings to prestigious top brass establishments in other parts of Europe could impose similar arduous leisure in cultural honeypots and city centres in Holland, Belgium, and Germany.

A ski-training complex in Norway still needed medical orderlies. What alternative did they have at weekends but to brush up their downhill slalom technique? RAF technicians working in India had to face the wilderness of Karachi and Bombay in their spare time. Subalterns in Tanganyika had to steel themselves for the austerities of Mombasa and Zanzibar.

It was not merely off-duty time that offered perks. If you spoke a bunch of languages, you could find yourself, with little or no officer potential yet discovered in you, with a pip or three on your shoulder, accompanied by the green flash which said 'Intelligence Corps'. Sometimes with a desk and a phone of your own. Thereafter you did little but read Russian newspapers all day. If you had a technical bent as well, you could crouch for hours listening to endless wireless messages being whizzed all over the place behind the Iron Curtain, or examining hundreds and thousands of reconnaissance photographs taken by Allied spy planes.

The very word 'intelligence' conjures up images of work that is rarefied, highly specialised, and frightfully hush-hush. However much truth lies in that impression, it seems fairly true to say that being in the Intelligence Corps, or its counterparts in the Navy and RAF, did not involve very much blood, sweat, and tears.

Another fast track to an unmilitary job was civilian professional qualifications. The obvious one here is a medical degree. If you were a qualified doctor, you did the most basic of military training before being awarded a captain's commission and told to go and ply your trade. Of course, it was the luck of the draw where you were going to be sent, but wherever it was, you were a doctor; you had an enviable rank; you could tell commanding officers what had to be done in the way of organising the battalion's life; and you had absolutely everybody at your mercy on the examination bed in your surgery.

Similarly, if you were an accountant, you could end up as the battalion paymaster, with, once again, a captain's commission. If there is anybody soldiers and sailors and airmen respect as much as the people who give them their medicine, it is the people who give them their money. Again, paymasters did not have to concern themselves with trenches and night patrols and servicing Land-Rovers and refuelling bombers.

A third profession which has always commanded respect, or at least wariness, is teaching. Everybody has been to school. Those posted to the Education Corps, therefore, got off to a good start. A teacher was a teacher. He had moreover the backing not of a headmaster but of the whole manual of military law. A sergeant's stripes helped too. Ed. Corps sergeants went everywhere; it could be very enjoyable. Or, if you were lucky, you could stay at home, and soak up local history teaching at the Tower of London.

A special case was the famous Services Russian course. If you were selected for that, you were sent to spend months in a spartan establishment called Cambridge University, where the irregular verbs and local hostelries vastly outnumbered the drill sergeants.

Or, finally, the Holy Grail of cushy numbers – or at least the cushiest that has come to the author's notice – was that enjoyed by a (rare) national service naval sub-lieutenant. He was a liaison officer in the Pacific. His job was to fly from warship to warship and be entertained in the wardroom. Poor man.

DOMESTIC LIFE

Ironing and barbering are the same necessary chores everywhere; it is only the circumstances that change.

A sergeants' mess off duty is a sergeants' mess off duty, regardless of country, creed, or colour. It was common in many places to use civilian labour for various menial duties. They could become familiar faces, and accepted as part of the furniture – and a trusted part of the furniture.

CHAPTER 27
Every Week the Same

There may be readers of this book who started willingly enough, and have got this far, but have felt their frustration, even annoyance, mounting the more they have persisted. They have, I hope, tolerated the slings and arrows of basic training, because everybody had to do it. It was, after all, the first shock, and the greatest shock. They were all in it together. If any of them forgathered in later years, the chances are that it was the stories of basic training that were most often exchanged, because that was the common ground; everybody knew about that. Everybody suffered.

But not everybody aspired, or tried, to become an officer. Fewer succeeded. So for many the account of officer training did not have the same urgency or grip – or, frankly, the relevance. By the same token, then, the same majority were not agog to read all about the later careers of these national service subalterns. An officer was an officer, and that was that. Separate ranks, separate facilities, separate privileges – separate lives. Who wanted to know more about them?

What about active service? There may have been some young men who yearned to get stuck into some real action, but they were unlikely to have been numerous. If they had been that keen, they would have signed on as regulars. So they did not feel left out when they heard of some regiment or other close to theirs which had been posted to Korea or Kenya or Cyprus. Being shot at by the Chinese? Facing a machete-wielding Mau-Mau terrorist intent on disembowelling you? Being blown up by a roadside bomb on the road to Famagusta? You could keep it.

Winning medals? You could keep that too. Who wanted to spend the rest of their life with one leg or half a lung? News of such exploits was more likely to provoke sympathy for the sufferer and disgust at the decisions of those who had brought it about than it was to engender envy or empathy.

So another chunk of the book would have little resonance for a large number of NS survivors.

Similarly, accounts of nice postings in Bermuda or Hong Kong or Jamaica would not be read with avid interest. And as for all those instances of cushy numbers – liaison officers knocking back double gins in the Marshall Islands, or eggheads loafing about the genteel courtyards of Cambridge University – well, lucky devils! Nothing like that ever happened to us. Nor likely to – not in a thousand years, never mind two.

Finally, if news got out of those who liked it so much that they decided to sign on as regulars, it would be met, not with envy, but with near-disbelief. They must be crazy.

Hence, then, the frustration, and the annoyance. When was this author going to get down to some common sense? When was he going to stop being bewitched by good stories, or lavishing his attention on those privileged persons who ended up smacking officers' batons against their calves?

As the Bible used to remind us, 'some there be that have no memorial'. A very large number, actually. In the case of National Service far and away the resounding majority of the two and a half million young men who did it. It is not given to everybody to be officers; all the rest have to be other ranks, otherwise there will be nobody to lead. Most people are not lucky enough to have had a comfortable time; if they have any sense, they will have realised how lucky indeed they were compared with everybody else. It is the majority that make up the bedrock of any human organisation.

So it was with National Service. Many of the jobs those countless thousands of young men found themselves doing may have seemed routine and humdrum, and, to them, they were indeed routine and humdrum. But, cumulatively, these young men must have been doing a worthwhile job; otherwise a cash-strapped government would have disbanded them.

Perhaps part of the tediousness arose not because of what was happening but because of what *might* happen. The Communists *might* spread further across Asia, and threaten the Empire in, say, Burma or India, as the Japanese had in the War. The terrorists in Cyprus *might* provoke a full-scale civil war. The Chinese *might* have another crack at Korea, or tackle Hong Kong. Finally, the wicked Russians *might* invade Western Europe. So a great deal of time, energy, and money had to be spent, not on action, but on readiness for action. And sitting around – just in case – can be boring.

However, it was not quite as bad as all that. Not every national serviceman spent his remaining twenty-one months as a private or an aircraftman or a plain seaman.

There were trades that could be learned, courses to go on, qualifications to be garnered. As a general rule, the Armed Forces were very good at teaching. Maybe not the sort of thing that most people were used to in secondary schools and sixth forms. But the Armed Forces were not there to teach you Latin and English Literature; they were there to show you how to defend your country, and, if necessary, run a war. Nevertheless, they could, and did, teach you to read and write if the primary school had let you down. No – what they were good at was technical subjects and physical skills. They taught you thoroughly, from A to Z, they made you work; they made you revise; and they tested you regularly. When they had finished teaching you, you generally stayed taught.

So suitable young applicants could go on courses to become physical training instructors, wireless telegraphists, cooks, drivers, military policemen, dog handlers, motor cyclists, fitters, signallers. There was specialist training for those who wanted to learn about medium machine-guns and three-inch mortars, or radar, or navigation. There were many others.

Some of these could lead to promotion – corporal, sergeant (though the author has never heard of a national serviceman who became a company sergeant-major or a petty officer). That had the added stimulus, of course, of an increase in pay from the derisory £1.40 a week that everybody began with.

A sizeable number stayed on at the depot after the end of basic training, and were incorporated into the basic training schedules of all those intakes that followed every six weeks thereafter. The meant a corporal's stripes too.

However, the fact has to be admitted that all these opportunities did not cater for everybody. There were plenty left who did not go on any prestigious courses or pin praiseworthy certificates on their wall. They became a duty driver, a kitchen assistant, an orderly room clerk, a messenger, a batman, a junior member of the provost staff (they could make the full circle, and appear as the formidable personage with the white belt who so impressed the new national service arrivals at the depot front gate). And *somebody* had to clean the depot toilets, light the boilers, and deliver coal to the Married Quarters.

It was more than likely that thousands of national servicemen did their share of jobs like this. Certainly a lot of them never got near a Bren gun carrier or a helicopter or an aeroplane or a destroyer.

Boredom therefore was an enemy, perhaps an unexpected enemy. To their credit, the Services tried to cope with that too, because their training philosophy, according to their public pronouncements, made a lot of fuss about maintaining morale. This took the form, largely, of games. Fine as far as it went.

But the fact still remained that there was spare time to be filled. Contrary to what the public might think, the Services did not do a particularly long day. Work normally finished at tea time on weekdays, and at lunch time on Saturday. Once basic training was over and once the later skills had been learnt, there was no cause to grumble about the number of leisure hours. (Active service of course was a special case.)

Weekends were the biggest bugbear. If you got away on a weekend pass, well and good. But if you had been posted to somewhere right off the map hundreds of miles from home, a thirty-six-hour pass was not much use. So there were those thirty-six hours stretching before you like some kind of wilderness. Many young men, used perhaps to company and gregarious weekend activities, and unused to entertaining themselves with reading or study or practical pastimes, found it difficult to cope.

It was all too easy to slip into apathy and inertia. For example, nobody made you get up on Sundays, so very often you didn't bother to get up. If others around you were sunk in the same slough of despond, it became doubly depressing. If your weekly pay had already been spent at the NAAFI or the pub in town, it got worse. Paradoxically, you almost welcomed Monday morning, because you knew that something would be happening, even if it was the same old thing.

That brought you back into the endless routine again. A driver had to take the Colonel to his brigade conference at the same time every Monday. A signaller had to send off the same routine messages at the same hour every day. A kitchen assistant had to get the same waste bins on to the same lorry, and the sanitary orderly had to get out his buckets and mops, because the need for that *never* changed.

This was a rut. And many young men found it difficult to escape it. Or at any rate to think beyond it. Once they had surrendered their mental independence like this, much of their time became spent working out how the routine chores, however small or unburdensome they were, could be avoided. They were swallowed up by the 'skive' philosophy.

One must always be on the lookout for 'a good skive'. How to smuggle some free cigarettes from the Sergeants' Mess bar, how to arrange deliveries of coal to the Married Quarters so that you had time to catch some tea and sympathy with a complaisant corporal's wife; how to stage-manage the leave passes that found their way on to the Chief Clerk's desk so that your mates got their weekend off; how to manipulate the timings on the duty lorry's work-sheet so that you could have an hour or two in town on a shopping spree while at the same time giving documentary proof of a frantic morning filled to bursting with official errands.

If you were stationed abroad – say, with the British Army of the Rhine or at NATO headquarters – there were perhaps more opportunities for creative 'skiving' which involved bartering Army supplies (sadly fallen off the back of a lorry) with local worthies, or cultivation of friendly relations with the local *frauleins* or *mesdamoiselles.*

It is perhaps for the above reasons that many national servicemen may not have particularly pleasant memories of their National Service. Or it may be that the laughter of reminiscence is tinged with scorn as times are recalled when the sergeant or the orderly officer or the 'snowdrops' (military police) were hoodwinked yet again.

Active service – to repeat – is a special case. There is nothing like active service, and in many cases those involved may not wish to revive memories of it, for obvious reasons. Some may have escaped physical injury, but were permanently scarred mentally. Such, sadly, is the case with all servicemen who go to war.

But ask an average national serviceman what he remembers about National Service, and you will get basic training – naturally. The bull, the drill, the rules, the sergeant-major. That is followed, quite often, by the fiddles, the rackets, the wheezes, the way they got round the regulations – the skives.

And one other thing is engraved indelibly on his brain. Whatever he thinks of the Armed Forces, no national serviceman ever forgets his number.

PERSONALITIES

A famous Army mnemonic – the ORQMS – Orderly Room Quartermaster Sergeant – in plain English, the battalion chief clerk. With his assistant, the Orderly Room Sergeant. Vital men to know.

A company sergeant-major – infinitely experienced, infinitely resourceful, impossible to pin down or to catch out. No officer with a grain of sense would make an enemy of him.

Sergeant-majors, contrary to popular legend, had a private life too, and were known to take their families on foreign postings. This one had six children. And he was a delight to work with.

A sergeant from the transport platoon – one of many who went into the (then) 'colonial' regiments. Usually educated in mission schools, and often very well educated too. This man's vocabulary would have done credit to a secondary teacher today, and his diction to a drama coach. And English, after his own tribal tongue and Swahili, was his third language.

CHAPTER 28
Where Do You Want to Go?

Perhaps it was the effect of the First World War, and the fact that the Napoleonic Wars were so far back in time, but people did not think of members of the Air Force or the Navy as 'cannon-fodder'. Trafalgar, where hundreds of men could die in a single broadside, was no longer part of the nation's folk memory. The victory was, of course, but not the casualties. Waterloo was a glorious victory too – along with Trafalgar, it constituted the foundation (along with the Industrial Revolution) of Britain's greatness throughout the nineteenth century, so that must have been all right.

No – it was the First World War which was the great icon of mass slaughter. In terns of sheer numbers, this was right. And it was the Army which had taken the brunt of the disaster. So people still thought of the Army as the place where you got killed most often and most inevitably. The figures for merchant shipping sinkings in the Second War, or the scale of casualties in Bomber Command, had not, in the 1950s, filtered through, or been allowed to filter through, to the nation's consciousness.

It was this perception, perhaps, which coloured the thinking of many young men when they considered which of the three Armed Forces in which they would prefer to do their National Service. One stresses 'prefer' of course; none of them *wanted* to do it. But, faced with an unavoidable Act of Parliament, it came to a choice of the least of three evils, as they saw it.

There was another popular perception too: in the Navy, you travelled, you saw the world, you had girls in every port; in the RAF, you roared off into the wide blue yonder, and you did wonderful things like loops and rolls, and brought the kite back to the jolly old airstrip in plenty of time to get round to the pub and flirt with the local talent. In the Army, you wore dull-coloured clothes and you dug trenches and you marched and you marched, and you ate all your meals out of all those ghastly billy-cans.

There was the element of romance and medal-winning too. The Navy conjured up images of young Jack Tar coming back home after sailing the seven seas and having lots of adventures, and carrying all sorts of exotic goodies and souvenirs in his kitbag and the pockets of his capacious bell-bottoms. With the Air Force, it was air aces and dog fights and Biggles and the Battle of Britain and the 'Glorious Few'. Films added their contribution: all those images of the loyal signalman bringing up the cup of cocoa to the steely-eyed skipper in his duffel coat on the bridge of the destroyer in the middle of the freezing night as they shadowed the *Bismarck*; or the Wing-Co. shouting 'Tally-ho' to the WAAFs at control as he adjusted his polka-dot muffler and pulled his goggles into place before peeling off towards all those squadrons of Heinkels and Dorniers.

Much more exciting than the Army. Besides, you stood much more chance there of being shot at. What was more, the Government was offering you a choice: when you went first to register, you were asked to indicate which of the three you preferred. So it stood to reason.

It may have stood to reason, but it did not stand to reality. The Army was much bigger than either the Navy or the Air Force, and its commitments were that much greater. National Service had been conceived as a way of allowing the Army to fulfil all its obligations towards home, imperial, and foreign defence and security while at the same time allowing all those who had been called up for the duration of the War to go home at last. As the pundits constantly maintained, you win wars with troops on the ground in the enemy's country; you don't win them with ships in his harbours or aeroplanes on his airfields.

So, when thousands of young men received their orders to report, it was, in over seventy per cent of cases, to a military establishment, and thousands of dreams were dashed.

To be fair, there was an alternative philosophy, which ran like this: in wartime, you are going to be shot at. If you were shot at in the Navy, there was all that water, and no matter how strong a swimmer you were, the Atlantic was stronger than you. If you were shot at in the Air Force, there was all that air, and nobody could fly an inch. So quite a lot of more sober young men reflected that they would prefer to have *terra firma* beneath them, if only to fall on.

But it didn't matter, because the majority were going to be put in the Army, whether they liked it or not.

It worked the other way too: the Navy and Air Force, it seems, were more choosy about the conscripts they took. To put it crudely, the Army expected you to be able to march, dig holes, and fire rifles, and maybe occupy a few towns. The Navy wanted sailors who could operate complicated equipment like gun turrets and radio control centres and navigation equipment and engine rooms. The RAF expected you to do most of that, and fly aeroplanes as well, and get to the target at night, and drop bombs in the right places.

To repeat, this was a crude simplification, but it did embody a truth which arriving national servicemen found unwelcome: if you did not have technical qualifications from civilian life, you were unlikely to make it into Navy blue or Air Force blue. Only just over a quarter got into the RAF, and only two per cent made it into the Navy. Over seventy per cent went into the Army, of whom four in ten went into the 'business' parts like the Artillery, the Armoured Corps, and the (inevitable) infantry.

PROVOST AND DISCIPLINE

A depot bugler. Why do military musicians so often look like Ruritanian commissionaires?

Provost Sergeant. As with many men involved in discipline, it often came as a surprise to others to discover that he had a family life.

RSMs, it seems, were the same the world over. This man exercised the same sort of authority over the African troops under him as British RSMs did with British soldiers. This RSM had a fearsome battle record too – Military Medal – and Bar.

The kings of panoply were the drum majors, and this one was no exception. He had a humble minion marching one pace behind him, carrying his great white gauntlets with gingerly care. At a snap of the drum-major's fingers, he leapt across the intervening pace and held them out as if he were presenting the Koh-i-Noor on a silk cushion.

CHAPTER 29
The Wide Blue Yonder

There was something special about the air. Everyone understood the land, took it for granted. They lived on it. A lot could live with the sea too. Even those who were only occasional travellers, and who perhaps feared the sea, at least appreciated that there was something there to hold you up, if only for a while. But in the air there was nothing. It defied logic, never mind gravity. There was something almost magical about it. Something devilishly cheeky about it too, as if one were taking on the Almighty, who, as everyone knew, would, if He had wanted us to fly, have given us wings.

The sea had its attractions of course. But they related to where a sea voyage could take you, rather than to the physical lure of the sea itself – all that water. The air on the other hand was hypnotic for some not because of where a plane could take you; it was hypnotic simply by being there. *Up* there. Looking down on the world. What better position of superiority could there be?

It was the image too. A young pilot in his service uniform, goggles, and fur-lined flying jacket, jumping down from his Spitfire, looked much more romantic that a double-breasted naval lieutenant in his baggy duffel coat with his binoculars round his neck and his chill-chapped hand clutching a cup of cocoa.

It followed then that a lot of teenagers, brought up on Biggles, and faced with the inevitability of National Service, decided that the RAF was for them. It would be making quite a good best of a bad job. Understandably too, they usually aspired to becoming pilots; there was nothing very romantic about being a fitter or a radar plotter. It was this group which suffered probably the highest percentage of disappointment when the time came.

For a start, sheer numbers were against them. Only about 25 per cent made it into the RAF at all, never mind into flying.

Those 'lucky' 25 per cent all had to go off to Padgate near Warrington, for the customary induction procedures. No regimental depots dotted around the country for the RAF; *everybody* went to Padgate, thousands and thousands of them. (Later in the 1950s this was changed to Cardington in Bedfordshire.)

Those who still harboured the flying ambition found the next hurdle on the receiving end of a stethoscope. The medical examination weeded out many more. It was not enough to be normally healthy; you had to have the reflexes of an Olympic mongoose and the eye of an eagle. And that was only physical health; there remained the small matter of the level of education. You didn't need many 'O' Levels to fire a rifle; you didn't half need them to fly an aeroplane – all that machinery and maths and navigation.

But first of course there was the routine part of the business – what every National Service recruit had to undergo, whatever the colour of his uniform. A medical was a medical wherever you went. A first 'service' hair-cut was just as traumatic in the Air Force as it was in the Army, and added to the indignity was the injustice of having to pay for it. The issue of kit varied only in the colour of the battledress; a pair of pants was a pair of pants, and a knife, fork and spoon was just that – no more.

Barracks accommodation was the same everywhere. Regimental depots had their ancient brickwork; RAF stations had their 'huts'. After the initial five days at Padgate or Cardington (punctuated, it seems, only by grinding fatigues – cleaning in the kitchens, delivering coal, presumably to fill in the day), recruits were shunted off to one of several basic training units, at Bridgnorth in Shropshire, Hednesford in Staffordshire, West Kirby in Cheshire, and Wilmslow near Manchester. Some stayed at Padgate or Cardington. They did eight weeks, which was slightly 'softer' than the ten or twelve in the Army.

As with the Army, they filled every minute with 'sixty seconds' worth of distance run' under the eye of a fierce instructor (often only a corporal), and tackled drill, basic weapon training, sessions in the gym, cross-country running, and the ubiquitous assault course. Instead of becoming acquainted with a platoon or a company or a battalion, they got used to being in a flight or a squadron or a wing. Their officers were not second lieutenants and majors and colonels; they were flying officers and squadron leaders and group captains. It wasn't the Regimental Sergeant Major who made them jump; it was the Station Warrant Officer. Like all their fellow-sufferers in khaki, they grumbled and they moaned, and they got fitter, and they passed out, in blue, just as their counterparts did in khaki.

A lucky few were selected for aircrew. It had helped if they had been in their school cadet force in the right colour, and even more if they had joined the RAFVR (RAF Volunteer Reserve). More still if they had done some civilian flying training, or had appropriate technical qualifications. If they hadn't, there was a series of intensive tests before a selection board.

It was no doddle. Failure rates were not low, and even after selection continued to be significant. Pilot cadets could expect an even higher rejection rate. And after the mid-fifties, there were hardly any National Service pilots trained at all. Teaching a pilot to fly a prop aircraft or an early jet (say, a Meteor or a Vampire) was one thing; preparing him to fly the later, more sophisticated machines like the Hunter and the Javelin was quite another. Indeed, it was out of the question. It would need a three-year commission to make it worthwhile.

National Service aircrew survived a little longer.

However, there were other things besides aircrew, and disappointed young airmen deemed to possess 'leadership potential' still had the chance to be trained as officers at the RAF OCTU (Officer Cadet Training Unit) at Jurby on the Isle of Man. They did twelve weeks, as opposed to the sixteen weeks for the infantry cadets at Eaton Hall and the gunners at Mons.

If they survived (and not all did), they became Pilot Officers specialising in a variety of technical roles – engineering, electronics, photographic interpretation, and so on. If they were lucky, they might get a foreign posting, most likely to NATO (the North Atlantic Treaty Organisation, protecting Western Europe from the scheming Russians) somewhere in Germany. Some officers' messes there could be quite palatial affairs.

Travel was available to other ranks as well, particularly if they could show aptitude for any kind of technical activity, and if they passed the RAF's quite daunting training courses. Wherever there were aeroplanes, there would be a need for countless legions of specialists to cater for all their needs – maintenance, repair, fuelling, electronics, navigation, armament, communications, and equipment so secret that nobody was supposed to know anything about it. They may not have flown aeroplanes, or even sat inside one, but they were around them all the time, and probably knew a great deal more about them than the pilots.

Work could take them to places like Aden, Egypt, India, Mesopotamia, Africa, Malaya, Cyprus, Jordan, Palestine, Korea of course, and scores of shore installations and remote islands all over the world.

However, it is suggested that only about half of all national servicemen ever saw a foreign country, and that statistic applied equally to the RAF. After all, there were plenty of squadrons all over the British Isles, and they needed back-up too. So, unless you knew somebody, you were as likely to be posted to the Orkney Islands as you were to Nairobi.

When all those airmen had been accounted for, there remained a residuum of national servicemen, as with the Army, who were not reckoned to have leadership potential, who did not have technical flair, and who were not up to passing complicated courses and regular exams.

Some found a niche as a drill instructor. They too had to survive an intensive course, but, if they did, they could return, often to the same place as the one they had started in, to do the same thing, only on the other end, so to speak. The RAF needed physical training instructors too. It needed mechanics. It needed operatives in a huge range of technical activities. The RAF never had as many national service NCOs as the Army, but those they did have made a useful contribution.

It needed medical orderlies, drivers, secretaries – any of which could lead to quite lofty postings as part of the staff of a very senior officer – distant flights to exotic places and plush accommodation in vast headquarters all over the world, with access to no end of luxurious local delights in off-duty hours.

At the bottom end there were all those other jobs which any service establishment had need of. So it was quite possible that a young man, full to the brim with Biggles and big hopes of life in the cockpit, would find himself as a barman in the officers' mess, serving drinks to other young men who had more 'O' levels and sharper eyesight then he had. Worse – for him – he could become a batman to one of those young men.

He could end up as a kitchen assistant, a sweeper, a cleaner, a 'general orderly', whatever term the station applied to the lowest form of animal life. It was not very inspiring. Small wonder they did not respond very positively to the suggestion of the personnel officer at the end of their service that they might like to sign on for another three years.

There was one chance left of – well, of something that was at least different. There existed a sort of military section of the RAF known as the RAF Regiment. It was created during the War to save the Army the trouble and expense of protecting RAF installations anywhere in the world. It continues to this day.

It also had a separate 'squadron' which engaged in ceremonial duties. It gave displays of drill, which, because they were totally silent after the original word of command, became world-famous. There may have been many soldiers who teased the RAF (and the Navy for that matter) about being pretty shambolic when it came to drill, but they would have to eat their words if they saw the Regiment's Drill Squad in action.

If a national serviceman could get himself into that, it could prove – well, interesting.

Finally, there was always the ultimate, the last word, the job that nobody could ever have foreseen, and whose genesis depended entirely on a random providence – plus, perhaps, a little naked opportunism.

One young aircraftman discovered that his passport to a better life was not a degree or a diploma; it was not membership of the RAF cadets when he was at school; it was not gallons of leadership potential or a Ph.D in radar engineering. It was membership of his school band. It was to enable him to get himself out of that most unavoidable and unpopular of all recruit activity – basic training.

He played the drums. At his recruits' training unit, there was, naturally, a passing-out parade every time a flight reached the end of its eight weeks. That meant that a band was needed. They couldn't afford the band of the Irish Guards, so they had to make do with a 'Drum and Bugle Band' to keep everybody at least in step. This young man was considered so indispensable that he was excused over eighty per cent of his basic training while the band rehearsed in a convenient hangar.

The authorities even laid on a lorry to take them to and from this distant hangar, and the NAAFI wagon visited them twice a day with goodies to keep them going. Now *that* is initiative.

GETTING TO KNOW THEM

If you kept your eyes and ears open, you began to notice that all African troops did not look the same. If you took the trouble, you found out something about the different tribes, and came to realise how important tribal differences were, differences which were carried into, and affected, their Army life.

On these page are examples of Mkamba, Kipsigis, Kikuyu, Luo, and Somali.

Characters – The ones who make life interesting anywhere.

This man ran a three-tonner, and threw his vehicle about the earthen roads like a crazed driver out of the film The Wages of Fear, *even when he was carrying a load of ammunition.*

A versatile young askari, who coupled his interest in the style of Lonnie Donegan (even if he had never heard of him) with an alternative career as the cinema projectionist. He also carried a pretty mean-looking spear when off duty.

CHAPTER 30

The Ocean Wave

The irony was that there wasn't much. The ocean wave, that is. The old song used to make the sad point that 'we joined the Navy to see the world, and what did we see? – we saw the sea'. But naval national servicemen didn't see an awful lot of that either. Not only did only about a half (of *all* national servicemen) manage to get abroad in the latter part of the NS period; the majority of *naval* national servicemen did not see much of the deck of a warship, never mind a foreign country.

There was further irony in the fact that England was supposed to be a sea power. Its early survival against its greatest European enemies – Spain, Holland, and France – had depended on its 'wooden walls'. Its rise to nineteenth-century supremacy had been due to Jack Tar far more than to Tommy Atkins. Britannia didn't rule the lands; it ruled the waves – for what that was worth.

Yet by the time National Service came along, the Royal Navy was far and away the smallest of the three Armed Forces. It was barely more than half the size of the Air Force, and only about a third the size of the Army.

It still boasted that it was the Senior Service, and to that extent it attracted more young conscripts than the other two. But yet another irony was that, frankly, it didn't want them – well, not that much. England had come a long way from the press gang. In the 1950s, it was the Army that had the most voracious appetite for recruits. To repeat, over 70% of all national servicemen went into the Army. Only 2% made it into the Navy.

The Navy, it seems, was not particularly short of regular volunteers, and anyway, during the 1950s, the Navy's complement of capital ships shrank by a third. And what it did need was personnel, for the most part, who could 'do' something, or who 'knew' something. The trouble was that the Army was the only service which expected its members to get to grips with the enemy close to, face to face, steel to steel. The Air Force bombed them or shot them down, and the Navy blockaded them or sank them. Small wonder, then – to put it at its most cynical – that it was the Army that needed the most cannon fodder.

So it was that the Air Force and the Navy set much more store by diplomas and degrees and apprenticeships and craft skills among its recruits – indeed went positively looking for them. Conversely, then, if you applied to the Navy and you did *not* have any of these pieces of paper to brandish, your hopes of getting in were not very often fulfilled.

One other thing might do the trick. If you had already shown interest in, and some kind of commitment to, the Navy, you were in with a chance. So membership of your school cadet force carried some weight. What carried more was some time given beforehand to the RNVR – the Royal Naval Volunteer Reserve. There were some resourceful, and lucky, young men who squeezed into the Navy after only about three or four weeks in the RNVR. Some had done it not because of love for navy blue, but because of the desire to avoid khaki (anything would be better than all that drill and marching and lugging heavy kit all over the place). But at least they had given the problem some thought, and they had done something about it.

There was a very small minority which could reasonably expect to get what they asked for – indeed, could get what they asked for without even the necessity to do several weeks of basic training, and without the often baffling process of officer selection. That was the medical fraternity. The Navy needed doctors and dentists like any other organisation. They could not afford to be so fussy any more about less-than-cut-glass accents or the wrong sort of school. A doctor was a doctor. He was rushed through a travesty of officer training, given a commission, and told to get on with it. No doubt the authorities took care that the resident sawbones was not put in an exposed place on a big parade. The Navy covered its face just a little by drafting them into the RNVR, as if to be able to make the excuse in case of trouble that they were 'volunteers' and not in the 'real' Navy – no connection with the firm next door.

Whatever the circumstances, the author has not heard of a single case of a young man who found himself called up for the Navy when he would rather have gone into the Army or the Air Force. It came down to the same thing in the end: whichever service they were summoned to, everyone found the process of initiation, induction, and basic training pretty much what it was for everybody else, given the obvious differences of the needs of each service. It hurt.

Where the Army recruits reported to a huge range of regimental depots spread all across the country, and the Air Force recruits had to go all to one place – either Padgate, or, later, Cardington (see Chapter 29) – the naval newcomers had a 'choice' of three – Chatham, Portsmouth, and Devonport, near Plymouth. There was another training centre at Corsham in Wiltshire. All below the line of the Thames – that meant a lot of travelling for a lot of recruits. They were all on land, but they all were given, and known by, the HMS nomenclature, as if they were seagoing ships – which must have taken some explaining to mystified family members.

The general consensus seems to have been that the standard of accommodation at these training centres was better than it was for the Army and Air Force. One Air Force recruit recalled that, as soon as his intake had left a particular set of huts, they had been officially condemned. Many Army recruits spent their twelve weeks in buildings judging by the names given to them (Alma, Inkerman, Balaclava) – which had been put up to house survivors returning from the Crimean War.

The new arrivals spent their time doing what recruits did in basic training in any 'military' establishment: drill, P.T., learning to clean kit, cross-country running, weapon-handling, and so on. Instead of swearing sergeants, they had swearing petty officers. For Regimental Sergeant-Major, read Master-at-Arms.

Like those in khaki and air force blue, they learned to live together, to make allowances, to become a member of a team; to take responsibility, to take punishment, to take chances, to take advantage, and (when the occasion presented itself) to take liberties. And to take the consequences. As with national servicemen everywhere, it was the making of many of them.

They learned to take opportunities too. The obvious 'opportunity' was the chance of a commission. The Navy only gave about 1,500 commissions during the NS period, but somebody had to get them. Those somebodies had to have 'volunteer' experience. In the RNVR, they had already learned a little seamanship, naval history, elementary navigation, drill, and so on. Perhaps more important, the Navy had higher expectations on the maturity front; nearly all national service naval officers were graduates.

They did their training on aircraft carriers and various shore bases, and were distinguished by three white stripes on each shoulder. In the Army and Air Force, they did it by means of white webbing flashes attached to the wings of the battledress collar. Either way, it set them apart, and made them obvious targets for any recruits who 'hadn't made it' or any NCOs who felt that they needed taking down a step or two. It made demands on their performance too; if they were going to show themselves as officer material, they had to do it better than anybody else. (Even when they were commissioned, they had a similar problem; all national service officers had to prove to the regulars, of whatever rank, that they were not just ex-schoolboy passengers but 'proper' officers.)

What helped them to prove their officer qualities, of course, was knowing something. That is, detailed and specialised technical skill – in, say, radar, electronics, navigation, and so on. This comes back to the Navy's intense interest in what a young man had done in his previous civilian life.

If a commission was out of their reach, or irrelevant to their ambition, there were plenty of roles for well-trained young men claiming civilian qualifications – in electronic, mechanical, and shipwright trades – and willing to build on those qualifications. The Navy kept a weather eye open for such people. There was a Radar and Technical School at Fareham, just outside Portsmouth. There was another 'HMS' shore unit at Petersfield in Hampshire to teach them about radio and codes.

As with the Army and the Air Force, that still left a residuum of ratings who did not become officers or radar technicians or divers or P.T. instructors or gun-turret experts. And as with the Army and the Air Force, there was a fair range of humdrum jobs waiting for them – storeman, wardroom orderly, NCOs' barman, sick berth attendant, electrician's mate, galley assistant, stoker, rust-chipper, and so on.

So, as with the Army and Air Force, boredom could haunt the hammocks as much as it did the barracks beds. Another cross all ratings bore was of course that of money, or rather the lack of it. Commissions and trade skills meant higher pay. If you were on the bottom rung of the ladder of rank, like aircraftmen and privates and riflemen and troopers and gunners, you received, to repeat, £1.40 a week. And you were even persuaded – nay, pressurised – to put some of that aside in a special savings account.

Quite apart from the restrictions on the *serviceman's* pocket, it could also mean hardship in his home. If he had been contributing to the household budget from his civilian wages, the loss of that contribution could mean severe shortage, particularly if his mother was a widow, more so if he had been the principal breadwinner. The problem was not confined, obviously, to the Navy. Whatever way you looked at it, and however much you stretched it, £1.40 was not going to go very far. There must have been some sad cases which had to be tackled (though not necessarily solved) by organisations like SSAFA (the Soldiers, Sailors, Airmen, and Families' Association).

So – given the obvious differences of colour of uniform, specialised trades, and the basic element involved (the sea, however distant it may have been) – the Navy presented problems similar to those of all national servicemen.

Perhaps a little surprisingly, the Navy also offered one slight hope of an escape just as the other two services did – the famous Russian Course. It seems that the authorities were taken by surprise by the Cold War. A lot of people had seen the Second World War coming, and in any case Europeans 'knew' about Germany (especially after the First World War), so there were a lot of German speakers available to do the work of listening and translating and decoding. But not many people knew about Russia (the Russians had seen to that), and Europe had been so taken up with defeating Hitler that it caught them on the wrong foot to discover that they now needed a whole new generation of Russian speakers – quickly – to deal with the Kremlin and its Machiavellian intrigues. Hence the Services Russian Course. Even the Navy got in on it. So smart young men with the slenderest of qualifications (like Anglo-Saxon or Latin) found themselves offered the option of learning Russian.

It was all in case 'the balloon went up' with Stalin. One Navy-trained Russian 'expert', at the end of his 730 days, received a travel warrant to report to Crail in Scotland, if it did. It was valid for ten years.

CEREMONIAL

Any Armed Forces unit has to go on show from time to time, and it could scoop up anybody, regardless of race, rank, status, or responsibility.

A group of British officers from a 'colonial' regiment, done up for a Queen's Birthday parade. Perhaps some of the paraphernalia may strike a modern observer as a mite silly. But times change. No doubt young officers of Nelson's navy would have chortled at the sight of doublet and hose.

An African warrant officer receives his Mention in Despatches from a lieutenant-general, the most senior officer around at the time. He was once sent on a signals course in England, and on the first day, to test him out, and not taking him seriously, they sent him a message at eight words a minute. He sent back the reply at sixteen. One learned respect serving with men like this.

It was common for 'colonial' regiments to send demonstration groups to public functions in England, largely because they were so colourful. In this case, it was a silent drill squad for the Royal Tournament.

An African battalion – both British and African personnel – trooping the colour on the Queen's Birthday parade.

CHAPTER 31
The Dividend

A lot of investment went into National Service.

The most obvious investment took the form of hard cash. Two and half million young men had to be fed, clothed, housed, equipped, and trained, over a period of about fifteen years. It is doubtful whether anybody has ever ventured to calculate the total cost, but the figure, whatever it is, must be noteworthy – even bigger than a banker's bonus.

Secondly, a good deal of hope and optimism went into it. The Labour Government of Clement Attlee could not be sure that their radical experiment would work. Looked at in cold blood, from this distance of time, it seems a huge risk: to sell a nation on the idea of conscription when the whole country was still panting from the exertion of fighting the biggest war in its history, when what everyone wanted was peace, rest, and normality. In fact it was not an experiment; it was an unavoidable necessity. If the men who had served throughout the War were to receive their discharge, and the responsibilities of the Armed Forces in peace-keeping and imperial security were to be sustained, there was no other way. Even so, the politicians had no means of knowing that the country would see it in that light.

Perhaps to everyone's surprise, the country did. At any rate National Service was introduced to succeed the extended wartime conscription which had persisted till 1947, and continued till 1963, when the very last national serviceman was demobbed. So all those young men, who may have grumbled, some of them bitterly, nevertheless invested a large amount of the benefit of the doubt. The attitude seems to have been: well, all right, we'll do it – but that's all. No political lobby, no civilian pressure group, no organisation of potential conscripts, mounted any kind of national refusal campaign.

Thirdly, the Armed Forces themselves – the regulars – faced with this huge influx of reluctant recruits, drew heavily on their reserves of professionalism, loyalty, and common sense to meet the nation's needs. It represented a massive investment of – for want of a better word – willingness.

Finally, a lot of time was invested too. Two years out of the lives of over two million young men. Some did only eighteen months, and some had to stay in for two and a half years (even more for a very few), but for the vast majority it was two years. Whichever way, it was a big slice out of a young life. And remember – nobody asked them whether they wanted to invest that time. But in it went.

Investment suggests a dividend. What did everybody get out of National Service?

The Government got a lot of cheap labour, for a start. The cost of all that feeding, clothing, housing, and training may indeed have been high, but as far pure labour was concerned, Her Majesty's ministers did rather well out of it. Pay in the early years was £1.40 per week, which, even for the late 1940s, was Scroogishly low. The average wage then was between £8 and £9. That is, a national serviceman received about 16% of the average pay packet. Towards the end of the NS period, he was getting only about 12%, so the Government was doing even better. And this, remember, was not for an ordinary nine-to-five job pushing a pen or swinging a shovel; it was a twenty-four-hour, seven-days-a-week business, which could involve not only exertion, but hardship, injury, and death.

Moreover, there was no danger money, no extra sickness payment. There was no demob suit at the end (which every wartime conscript could look forward to), and no gratuity either. No medal. No monument. And certainly no pension.

The Government got the service they wanted too. As remarked above, there was no nationwide protest, and no more than the usual percentage of avoidance, shilly-shallying, and pure desertion than one would expect in a professional army. Very good service too, by and large. National servicemen performed no worse in action than their regular counterparts. Some were decorated – the MM, the MC, the MBE. One received a DSO.

So their lords and masters asked for two years, and two years is what they got. But that, for the most part, was all they got. It seems that only a small portion of conscripts went on record as saying that they *liked* National Service. To be fair, only a similar portion said that they hated it. The vast majority accepted it, lumped it, made the most of it, did their best so far as their natural talents allowed, and looked forward to the 730th day – the last day. Not many of them succumbed to the siren songs of the personnel officer who interviewed them towards the end and suggested that they might like to sign on for another three years as regulars. No. Enough was enough.

What about the Armed Forces themselves? The regulars, the professionals, the ones who would still be there when all the conscripts had thankfully taken themselves off. Nobody had asked them, any more than they had asked the conscripts. The regulars, over a period of about fifteen years, had the task of taking two and half million unwilling young men straight from the streets and fields, and turning them, in a remarkably short time – as low as eight weeks in the RAF – into passable soldiers and sailors and airmen.

It is fashionable, in memoirs of an institution like National Service, to concentrate on the recruits. After all, it was they who were getting the shock treatment. That was where the drama was, where the tall stories came from. All the books about National Service known to the author were written from the recruit's point of view, from the receiving end.

What about those who were dishing it out? Did any regular sergeant or station WO write a book about National Service? Unlikely. To them, it was just another job. And, since they were professional, they did that job to the best of their ability.

It must have been hard for those long-servers with wartime experience. Teaching spotty-faced, pigeon-chested conscripts how to present arms was a long way from facing a Panzer division in an Ardennes winter or a Japanese ambush in Burma, or, worse, a Japanese prison camp.

They did indeed have to invest a lot of willingness. But, being human (despite all those national servicemen who became convinced that they were not), they took pride in what they were doing, and were just as pleased as their platoon or their section or their company or their squadron when the passing-out parade went well.

To their surprise, many of the young men they trained became instructors themselves. Indeed, when the Army found recruitment of regulars difficult from time to time, they came to rely on a large number of National Service NCOs. Some National Service officers too showed levels of leadership and humanity which had not always been evident among the ranks of the public-school, privileged, silver-spoon young men who had regarded a commission as their birthright. So there was profit there too.

What about all the rest who passed through the hands of the much-remembered (and often much-maligned) regulars? The rank and file – the ones who did *not* get a commission, the ones who did *not* become NCOs. What about them? It is true that many found themselves in unspectacular, humdrum, repetitive, totally predictable, and frankly boring jobs for their remaining twenty-one months.

But many of that remainder, when placed in circumstances which demanded more of them, in difficult places all over the world, came well up to scratch. It is often claimed that the British soldier – at any rate for the two or three decades after the War – was the finest human fighting unit in the world. Some may take issue with that verdict. But, if it is true, some of the credit for that must go to national servicemen.

Which brings us round to the national serviceman himself. He put two years of his life into the system. What did *he* get out of it? What did it do for him?

Well, whether he enjoyed the process or not, it certainly made him fitter, stronger, and tougher. Early to rise (and, mostly, early to bed), the great outdoors, regular exercise, regular meals, and the adrenalin stoked by travel, challenge, and adventure, could not fail to develop an adolescent's physique. Those who came to the military life after three years' dissipation in college bars and clubs probably found the change even more beneficial, if slightly more painful.

It made them smarter too. Many came to realise that dress, grooming, and general appearance were important. They started to take pride in how they looked and how they bore themselves and how they moved. For the rest of their lives, some of them would not leave the house with dirty shoes or twisted laces. The simple act of standing up straight did wonders for their self-respect.

Being forced to live with so many others, in such close proximity, taught them tolerance and flexibility. They learned to make allowances. Striving together towards a common goal taught them teamwork. They became aware that there was such a thing as *esprit de corps.* They never thought the day would come when they would be pleased, much less proud, of what they accomplished, say, on a passing-out parade, but come it did. They began to take pride in belonging – to a platoon, a company, a squadron, a regiment, a ship; and there is plenty of evidence to show that they were prepared to stick up for their unit, with their voices and sometimes with their fists. Again, they would never have dreamed, when they first walked through the barracks gate, that such a thing could come to pass.

They made the discovery of that peculiarly male relationship which the Forces are especially adept at creating – comradeship. Some confessed to being nearly overwhelmed when the last day came and it hit them for the first time that all those familiar faces were about to disappear from their lives. A few said that, in the turmoil of the moment, they came near to signing on as regulars.

They were young. Perhaps this was the first really strong human emotion to hit some of them. They were totally unprepared, and they were bowled over by it.

Many had never been away from home before. Doting mothers had done everything for them. The barrack room soon dealt with that. It was not only bulling boots and cap badges; it was cleaning, darning, ironing, sweeping, polishing, cleaning toilets. Those who had been away – particularly those public school schoolboys who had survived homesickness and dormitory bullying and spartan meals for seven years – enjoyed a distinct advantage.

There were peripheral benefits too, like learning to manage a budget. All a national serviceman's cleaning materials – polish, blanco, dusters – had to be bought out of his £1.40 a week. Of course, those fond parents were bound to help if they could, and no doubt those who were able to get home on a weekend pass had Mum or Dad to pay their train fare. If Mum or Dad did not pay the fare home, they learned to hitch-hike. Young men in uniform were a common sight on the roads in those days, and drivers were usually well-disposed to offering lifts to khaki and blue. Nevertheless, what today's society calls the learning curve was steep. There was so much of it too. But every step taken was another step up the staircase towards self-reliance and self-sufficiency.

The higher they went, the more they grew in self-confidence. When they returned home and looked at the weedy civilians around them, they felt different. Those who moved on to university gazed in surprise at the freshmen who had gone up to college straight from school; they looked so immature.

Nor did they have to wait till they went to university to learn something. The Forces could, and did, teach you a trade – many trades in fact. And, as has been remarked before, when the Forces taught you anything, they usually taught you very well; they taught you from A to Z; and, when they had finished teaching you, you stayed taught. A lot of NS survivors took those trades into civilian life, and made careers out of them.

Some even owed their literacy to the Forces. There were lessons in reading and writing. For those without it, there could hardly be a more precious gift with which to start you on the road. There were few other institutions outside the orphanage which could take you in with nothing to your credit, and house, feed, clothe, teach, and train you.

So, for a lot of young men who had had little sense of purpose as teenagers, life in the Forces provided eye-openers, opportunities, possibilities. It raised their sights. Not only did it show them what they were capable of doing; it made them aware that there were so many things waiting to be done. Like all good education systems, it made their pupils discontented. They wanted to 'get on'. They returned to civilianism after their two years, no longer prepared to tolerate the empty, listless life they had endured before. The old rails they had once run on had far too narrow a gauge, and led nowhere.

Some national servicemen, perhaps somewhat to their surprise, found the military life to their taste, and signed on as regulars. They took up specially-tailored three-year commissions, which of course carried the attractions not only of extra pay, but the prospect of pensions as well; others, of all ranks, committed themselves even further. A few reached very high rank – brigadier, air commodore, major-general (in the Marines), a lieutenant-general, and two field marshals (one of them became the professional head of the whole British Army).

However, even if every conscript had known that two field-marshal's batons were hidden in their knapsacks, not all of them would have had much to say for the whole institution. The above recital of the many benefits that accrued from two years in uniform for so many of them should not mask the fact that it was not like that for everybody.

A few, as already indicated, hated the whole thing. Others had made up their minds that it was going to be awful, and duly proved it to themselves. Many of those who went overseas had the adventure of foreign travel for the first time in their lives, but they soon found it curdled by the searing reality of active service, whether on patrol against terrorists in Malaya or Cyprus or Kenya, or in full-scale war in Korea, or in a half-cock war in Suez.

Nearly 400 died. Hundreds more were wounded (some crippled for life). Hundreds more again died in accidents – with loaded weapons, vehicle collisions, air crashes, and so on. Some of those who returned found themselves scarred psychologically for ever. A new phrase was seeping into the language – post-traumatic stress disorder.

Two more rare occurrences accounted for further casualties.

In the mid-fifties, thousands thought they had been given the posting of a lifetime to a South Seas paradise. They were sent to build installations on Christmas Island, in preparation for a test series of nuclear explosions. The biggest one was in 1957, when the first hydrogen bomb was detonated. This, and others, were designed to test not only the weapons themselves, but the effect on the human frame, with or without protection. The soldiers themselves knew little about radiation, much less the level of the damage it could do. The trauma and disease and wearisome litigation was to continue for decades.

At round about the same time, the Government embarked on a run of tests into the common cold and the effects of certain types of poison gas. Volunteers were asked for, to act as guinea pigs. They were assured that it would be quite safe. They were offered a bonus and a few days' leave. Some of those who took it up were national servicemen.

One man provably died because of the experiments. Many others have suffered ever since from a hideous roster of complaints, but it was decades before the mask of secrecy began to be lifted, and the story is not over yet.

It should be clear even from this far-from-definitive list of effects that there is no simple verdict on National Service. It was so varied, it involved so many young men, in so many different roles, in so many parts of the world, that there is no snap judgment which would be worth anything. It generated so many emotions – shock, disbelief, fatigue, worry, fear, horror, laughter, loneliness, misery, affection, pride, exaltation – the list is almost endless. And they could often follow very closely on each other's heels.

If there is any general agreement, it might be that it was a life-changing experience for nearly everybody. Whether the change proved permanent is open to question; one would have to study the lives of two and half million young men.

It was certainly a life-*marking* experience. Certain things about National Service you simply do not forget. All national servicemen have plenty to talk about when they assemble.

Is it any easier to judge today, with the wisdom and perspective of hindsight? Unlikely. It was so long ago; people attempting to judge it now would be unable to come to a balanced decision because they are not attuned to the attitudes and values of the time. It was simply a phenomenon of the decade and a half after the War and that was that.

It came, it flourished, and it has gone. It was needed at the time, and it served its purpose. It is no more likely to come back than so many of those other phenomena of other times, which had their day and their uses – mangles, quill pens, steam trains, battleships, oil lamps, and the abacus.

RELAXATION

Dressing up for Christmas – as one does on the Equator. The Lord of Misrule is in charge, as he is in so many Forces units at that time.

On Sundays, the English gentleman digs his garden. Or a bored subaltern plants flowers in the Officers' Mess garden – as you do.

Everyone wrote home – in the prehistoric days before satellites and mobile phones and emails. And then you may have to turn to and put on Number One uniform for a big parade.

The more active (or more bloodthirsty) engaged in dubious sports like pig-sticking.

With plenty of wide open spaces, nobody complained much if you took up a noisy musical instrument. Very few people can boast of having been able to practise in front of a 15,000-foot mountain.

CHAPTER 32
Bring Back National Service

How you view your past depends upon how old you are. Two years when you are eight make a quarter of your life; two years when you are forty make only a twentieth. If you were a schoolboy in the 1940s, you would have viewed the Boer War as ancient history, and it was only forty years before. A radio presenter today can blithely talk about the 1980's as if they were the Middle Ages, but to a survivor of National Service, they were almost yesterday, because, to him, they were only one decade out of seven or eight.

The author remembers a conversation he had in about 1960 on the subject of Winston Churchill. Being a historian, he (the author) gaped at the sudden realisation that this statesman, who was still alive, had been present at the last British cavalry charge in history – the Battle of Omdurman, in the Sudan, in 1898. Churchill was there; *he rode at Omdurman.* Sixty years before.

Now look at this book. It is commemorating the demise of National Service fifty years ago. And it began in 1948, over *sixty years ago.* Are people going to gape too at the author, and gasp at the thought that he was *there* all that time ago? *He actually did National Service.* Can he look forward to being wheeled out in fifteen or twenty years' time as some kind of museum piece, like the final survivors of the First World War, who amazingly lived to see the twenty-first century?

Of course the survivors of the *Second* World War will be wheeled out first, but, when they have gone, it will be the turn of all those lads from pit and palais, from college and workshop, from shop counter and factory floor, who had to give it all up and do their two years. Eager young interviewers, at present barely out of rompers, will thrust microphones under their beaky noses and pretend to marvel at their reminiscences of bull and blanco as if they were chronicles of the decline and fall of the Roman Empire.

The chances are too that many of those two and half million young men will be around longer than the survivors of the two wars. People are living longer nowadays. And, like all survivors of a traumatic experience, they will keep their memories in good repair. They may not be able to remember what their wives asked them to do half an hour ago, but they will all be able to recall endless details of their two years – and, more often than not, be more than willing to recount them.

The call-up, the medical, the first day, the issue of kit, the washing facilities, the food, the barrack room, and of course the first NCO – and a thousand other things – will be as fresh and as sharp as a newly-opened tin of paint.

They will have their own repertoire of stories – funny, sad, moving, tall, doubtful, unlikely, and downright impossible. They will all be eager to recount the things they got up to – the tricks, the jokes, the wheezes, the skives, the rackets. They will purvey what by now have become legends about their corporal, their platoon sergeant, their RSM, their Station WO, their CPO, their Commanding Officer. They will fish down from a dusty shelf the actual spoon they were issued with on that first distant day. They will live yet again their travels, their hardships, their adventures, their narrow escapes. (The only reticent ones are likely to be those who actually saw the realities of war, or at any rate went on active campaigns in uncomfortable parts of the world. Many of *them* may well have spent the intervening years trying to forget.)

One irony of this situation is that the dazzle of the memory of those two years all that time ago can blind us to what has happened during the fifty or sixty years which separate us from that memory.

Nobody could ever produce a full account of all the changes that have taken place between the National Service Act of 1948 and the fiftieth anniversary of the demise of that National Service – 2013. But a few examples will produce enough reminders, and those reminders, taken together, will produce, it is hoped, a sharp appreciation of the gap that now separates us from the young privates and gunners and guardsmen and ratings and aircraftmen and fusiliers and riflemen and sappers and troopers who walked so obediently into the barracks and depots and shore stations in response to the buff envelope they had all dreaded receiving.

Obedience is perhaps one of the key words in this. Young people today would be amazed if they knew the extent of the capacity for obedience of the young in the 1940's. When one reads of the extent to which the young generation in the USA were prepared to go in order to escape 'the draft' only twenty years later, in the 1960s, the distinction becomes even sharper. In the 40s and 50s nearly all those called up simply went. They accepted it as something which had to be done; protesting about it did not come into it. Even when they were later sent to uncomfortable places like Korea or Cyprus or Kenya or Suez, there seems to have been little mutinous criticism. Many had no clear idea why they were even there. They just blamed 'them' for arranging it. It was merely something else to grumble about.

The War too is very relevant. The country was less than a decade away from the worst and biggest war in human memory. Hardship, danger, grief, deprivation, fear, discomfort, shortage had all been part of life for the best part of six years. A whole country had learned to accept what the War flung at them – uprooting, evacuation, bereavement, rationing, putting up and making do. The young men who came to National Service had learned acceptance and stoicism and lumping it pretty well from the cradle. Some came from such poor homes (many slums had been conveniently bombed, but there were plenty left) that they found the barracks no great discomfort. They probably had more room than they had had all their previous lives, crowded four or five to a bedroom. Some had never slept in a bed by themselves. Many had lived on such poor food (and everybody had had to put up with food rationing, which went on for years *after* the War) that they found the regular meals in the Army and the Navy and the Air Force much more than barely eatable; they were welcome.

So the generation nurtured and shaped by the War coped well enough with National Service – after the initial shock, that is. Barely a decade after high-explosive bombs, and nights in a corrugated iron shelter in the garden, and a four-ounce meat ration each week, and hardly any private cars on the road, and utility furniture; after the period known as 'Austerity' just following the War, when things if anything got worse (rationing certainly did) and shortages never seemed to diminish, a mere sergeant-major and a tin of blanco and a depot bugler at dawn were no big deal. To repeat, they were a shock, but they were a shock that one soon came to terms with, like being bombed out or playing cowboys and indians on rubble-strewn gaps in the rows of houses.

The second feature of life then which would strike a modern observer as – well – quaint was the lack of sophistication and knowledge of the world. Where to begin to explain. Let us try with television. In the late 40s very few households owned a set. If they did, it was a minute object almost drowned in the great container of timber that was deemed necessary to house it. It was as big as a large chest of drawers, but the screen was barely six or eight inches across. It was such a rarity and a novelty that neighbours and friends would come round for the evening 'to watch the television' as an evening's social entertainment. (It would be interesting to know when the word 'telly' was coined.)

There was however a great rush to buy TV sets in order to be able to watch the Coronation in June, 1953, and that might have improved things.

However, the early programmes were scheduled normally for the afternoon and evening, and usually shut down well before midnight. There was only one channel till the mid-50s, when ITV made its much-criticised appearance. Programme content was pretty decorous – live dramas, quizzes, game shows, sport commentaries and children's fare of course, and not much else. Compare that with what is on offer today.

There simply was not the amount of knowledge available. Think of the extent of world geography, for instance, that can be seen in modern documentaries and travel programmes. There was none of that in 1948. In any case, there would have been no point in whetting viewers' appetites, because most people could not afford to go there. For several years after the War, in order to stop pounds leaking abroad into other countries' economies, there was a limit to what a citizen could spend. Believe it or not, nobody was allowed to spend more than £25 – in a year.

So young men's views – everybody's views – were limited, to say the least. Nowadays a lot of young people would have had holidays in places where national servicemen went to serve – and possibly fight, even die: Malaysia, Kenya, Cyprus, Egypt.

It was the same with food. To repeat, we were only a decade away from wartime food rationing – and from supplements like corned beef, whale meat, dried egg, and orange juice for babies. Bananas disappeared from the shops for six years. Dammit – we didn't see all that much of *English* food, never mind foreign food. No Italian restaurants, no Chinese restaurants, no Vietnamese, Danish, Thai, Bangladeshi, nothing. And there wasn't all that much on offer in English restaurants either.

There were no ramparts of cooking literature in bookshops. Olive oil was something you warmed up and poured in to ease earache. Coffee came out of a bottle labelled 'Camp'. Rice was something you made puddings with. Pasta was probably some kind of building material. And so on and so on.

We were equally insular in our attitude to other countries – and their inhabitants. Other people were classified under headings like Frogs, Wogs, Wops, Eyties, Jerries, Yids, Yanks, Nips, Chinks, and Dagoes. It was not so much racist prejudice as pure ignorance. We learned quickly enough when given the chance. National servicemen, when posted abroad, soon picked up a liking for rice, curry, pasta, ouzo, and anything else that was on offer. They proved equally adaptable too when it came to serving with African and Indian regiments.

What all this is endeavouring to show, perhaps in a ponderous way, is that we were different then. We were more obedient, more conformist. And we knew far less of the world, tucked away in our tight little island. What we did know was that the British were best, and we were not particularly interested in arguments or evidence to the contrary. Besides, we had won the War, which proved it.

Another example to drive this point home – if indeed it needs driving by now – is the absence of good causes so common today. Atomic weapons had only just arrived – at Hiroshima and Nagasaki – so there were no anti-nuclear demonstrators yet pushing prams to Aldermaston. There were no 'save the planet' movements, largely because nobody had told us that it was in danger. There were no crusades to save the whales, save the badgers, save the tigers, the elephants, the white seals, the battery hens, the rain forest, the ozone layer, and the donkeys in Algeria. If you were green then, it meant that you were a bit wet behind the ears.

For six years there had indeed been one Good Cause – and a very 'good' one. It was called 'Winning the War'. People could see the sense in that, and had been prepared to make sacrifices for it. The habit of service and sacrifice persisted for some years afterwards, and goes some way to explain why National Service was accepted. With grumbling, but it was accepted. We didn't know any better. We had won a war; we had a reputation to defend, and we were proud of it; and we still had an empire.

The 1950s saw all that begin to evaporate. The crisis came with the Suez disaster. By the 1960s not even the Government were inclined to take National Service seriously, and some of the Cabinet had not wanted it in the first place. The Navy stopped national service recruitment altogether two or three years before the Army and the RAF.

So attitudes were changing, and these were more important than the 'obvious' differences. One could no doubt fill pages with details of the material things that we didn't have in the '40s and '50s. The most 'obvious', perhaps, were mobile phones, computers, and credit cards. They are so much part of the very bloodstream of the human race today that it might be difficult for somebody younger than, say, twenty-five to imagine a world without them. Good God! How did they manage?

Well, we did. And we managed, too, without regular air travel, the zip fly, the pill, CDs, DVD's, supermarkets, pop music charts, discos, futons, gay marriages (you could go to *jail* for that), paracetamol, hovercraft, duvets, microwaves, delicatessen counters, anoraks, hospital scans, supertankers, high-speed trains, combine harvesters, motorways, pubs open all day, twenty-four-hour news, phone-ins, sit-ins, love-ins, and just about everything-ins.

And we used to marvel too, at what our parents' generation had been without. They – poor souls – had had to struggle through life without radio (till the 1920s), the Welfare State, washing machines, vacuum cleaners (till the 1930s), biros, central heating (so did many of us), the NHS, and long-playing records. We regarded them as a completely deprived generation.

And our grandparents' generation had been deprived yet further. There seems to be a sort of inverted logic which dictates that the greater the deprivation, the greater the population's preparedness to tolerate universal military service. The National Service generation went, maybe not like lambs, but they went, to do their two years. Their parents went in their millions to 'do their bit' in the Second World War. And their grandparents queued up to volunteer in 1914 (not only in England, but in every major country in Europe) to face what turned out to be the horrors of trench warfare, artillery barrages, and the medium machine-gun – and they stuck it out.

Follow this argument in the reverse direction, and you reach the conclusion that today's younger generation, steeped in goodies, made aware of everything (so they think) by the telly, and omniscient (so they think) thanks to the internet, would not tolerate a return of National Service. They simply wouldn't wear it. And no politician would dare to open his mouth in favour of it. Look at the national soul-searching that wracked the country on the pro's and con's of going to war in Iraq or Afghanistan. Imagine another National Service Act of Parliament which decreed that every able-bodied young man would be called up at eighteen, to serve for two years – even a year – even six months – in case of other similar wars to be fought, or trouble-spots to be 'monitored'. The final 'justification' – defending the empire – can hardly be mentioned, when 2012 sees countries as disparate as Scotland and Jamaica talking about 'independence'.

That is as may be. The author does not offer this as unbreakable logic. There was the small matter of the Falklands War in 1982, when a generation of young uniformed personnel – of both sexes and all three services – moved Heaven and earth to get themselves selected to be sent to the South Atlantic. So there is no definitive answer.

No definitive answer at any rate on that front. But perhaps there might be on another.

No government, like the one at present, is going to contemplate paying for a new generation of national service, when they claim that the country is reeling from the effects of the greatest deficit since the War; when they are cutting jobs and grants and services and hand-outs on every side; when the truncated Armed Forces are complaining that their equipment is insufficient or inadequate or out of date, and warning that the time is fast approaching when they will not be able to fulfil the commitments still required of them.

Consider too the matter of simple arithmetic. At the height of National Service, 6,000 young men were conscripted every fortnight. That is 156,000 every year. Quite apart from the problem of housing, feeding, and clothing them, there was the greater problem of training them. Who would be available to do it now? With troops and other personnel in

Iraq, Afghanistan, and Kosovo (and no doubt other places that the author has overlooked), and a grand total of all the Armed Forces coming to barely 160,000, how would all these 156,000 young men be trained? (That number would probably be higher now, because of the rise in population.)

It would seem, then, that the bar-room pundits, who know the answer to everything, may be slightly off beam when they put forward their remedy for society's current curse of yobs and layabouts and hoodlums and junkies: 'Bring back National Service'.

For one thing, as one hopes has been demonstrated, 'they' couldn't, even if they wanted to – and they don't. For another, younger generations have been denigrated before, but young Tommy did his bit well enough in two World Wars, and his sons and grandsons did their bit in National Service without too much trouble. Who knows? Perhaps, faced (God forbid) with another crisis, those yobs and layabouts might do theirs.

LEAVE

Fate (or the Forces) had a habit of dumping you in distant places, but often quite interesting places (with 'sights' often not too far away). It would have been a pity not to try and see some of them.

Nairobi Cathedral

The Equator Inn, Nairobi – the authorities had a very civilised habit of accommodating pupils on their Swahili course in this most acceptable hostelry.

You could sit on Portuguese cannons, or bask on tropical beaches, or sample a tropical twilight as the mood took you. You had better; you were not likely to get such a chance again.